SCIENCE FICTION ILLUSTRATIONS

Jean-Pierre Normand

SCIENCE FICTION ILLUSTRATIONS

A Black Coat Press Book

Copyright © 2009 by Jean-Pierre Normand.

Visit the artist's website:
http://www.jeanpierrenormand.com

Visit our website at www.blackcoatpress.com

ISBN 978-1-934543-79-5. First Printing March 2009. Published by Black Coat Press, an imprint of Hollywood Comics.com, LLC, P.O. Box 17270, Encino, CA 91416. All rights reserved. Except for review purposes, no part of this book may be reproduced or transmitted in any form or by any means, electronic or mechanical, including photocopying, recording, or by any information storage and retrieval system, without permission in writing from the artist or the publisher. Printed in the United States of America.

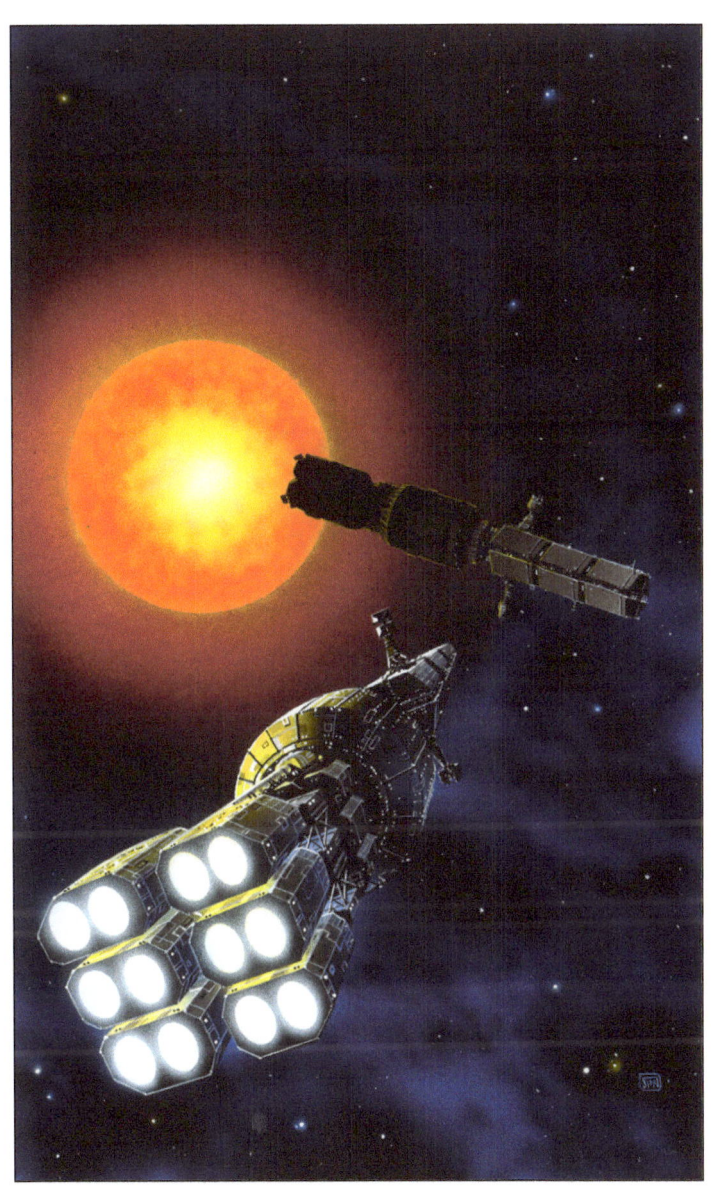

Betelgeuse

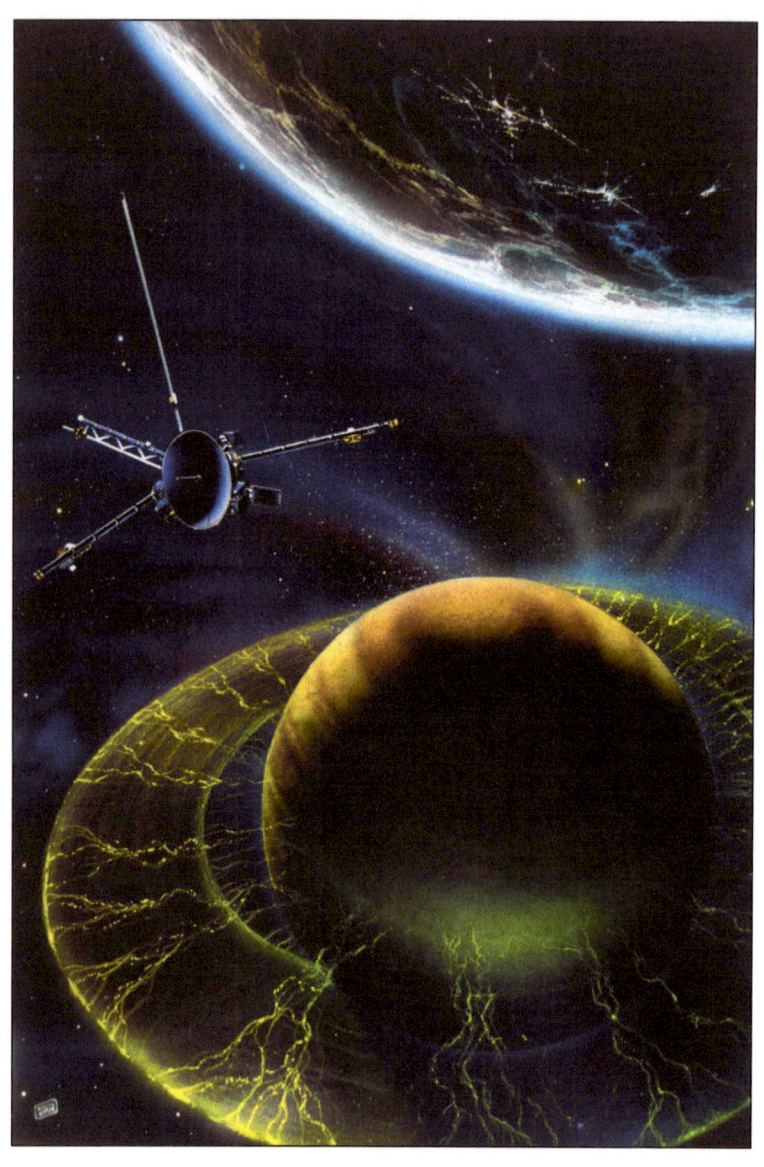

Orbit 1

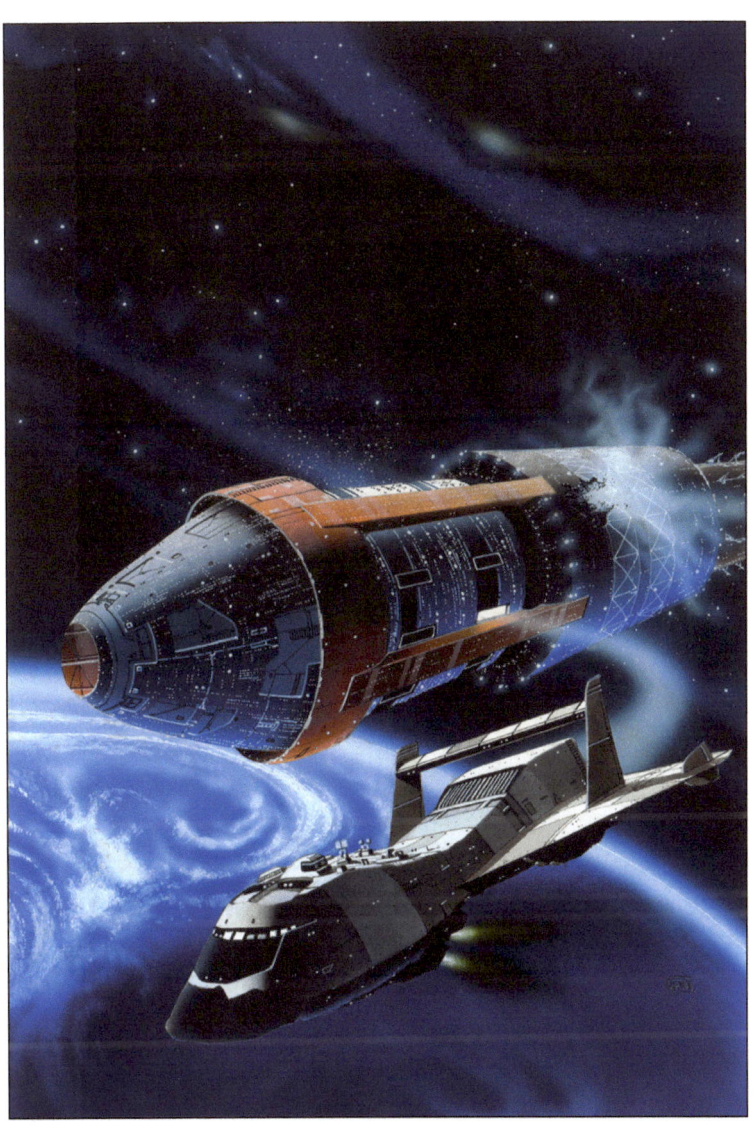

Evacuation

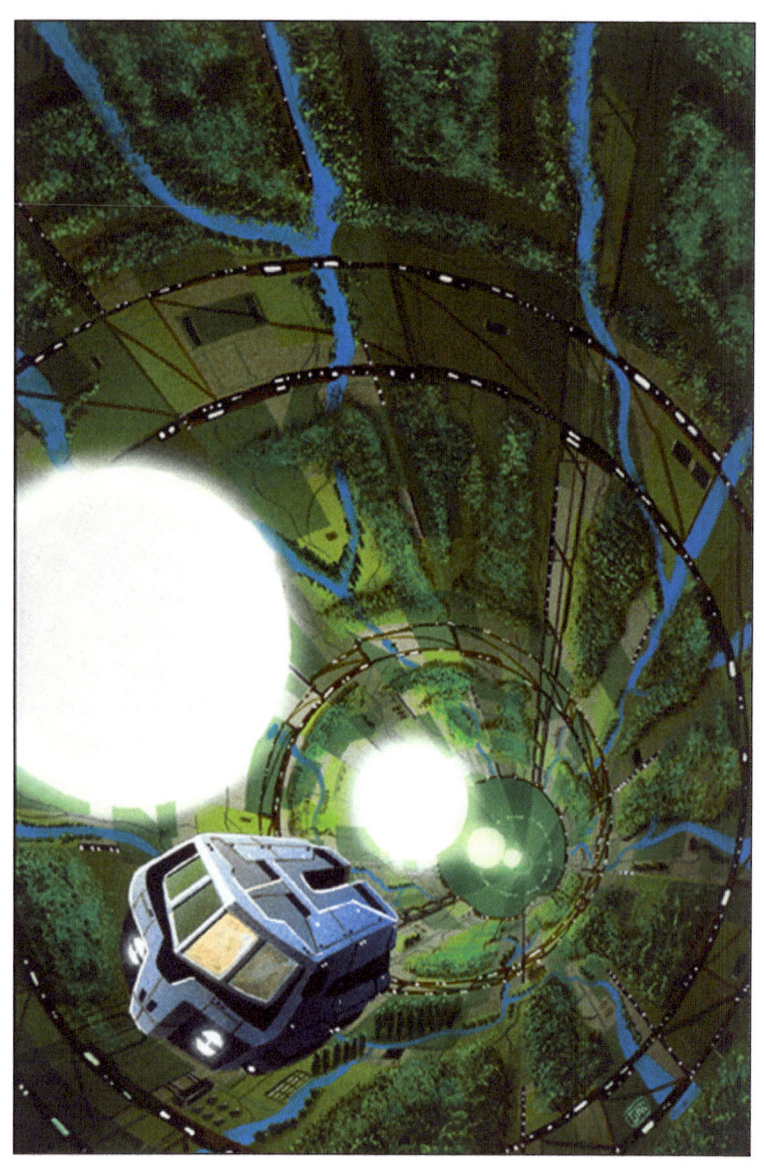

Fomalhaut

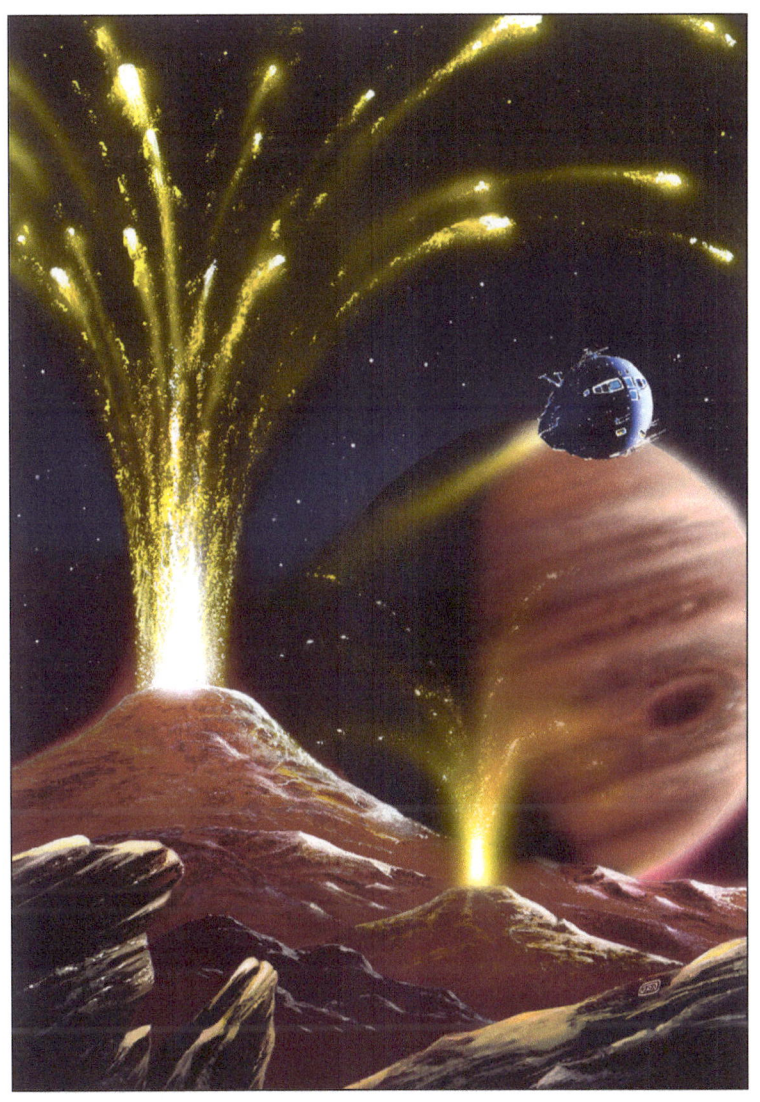

Io

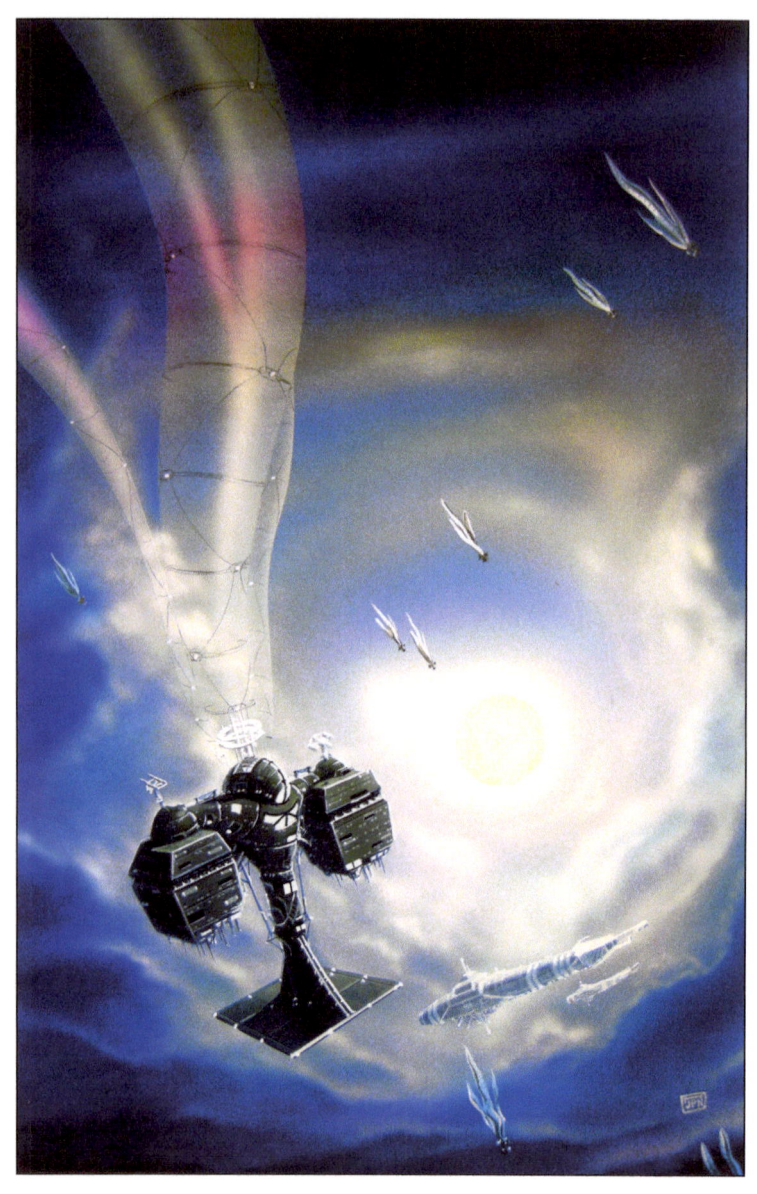

Probes

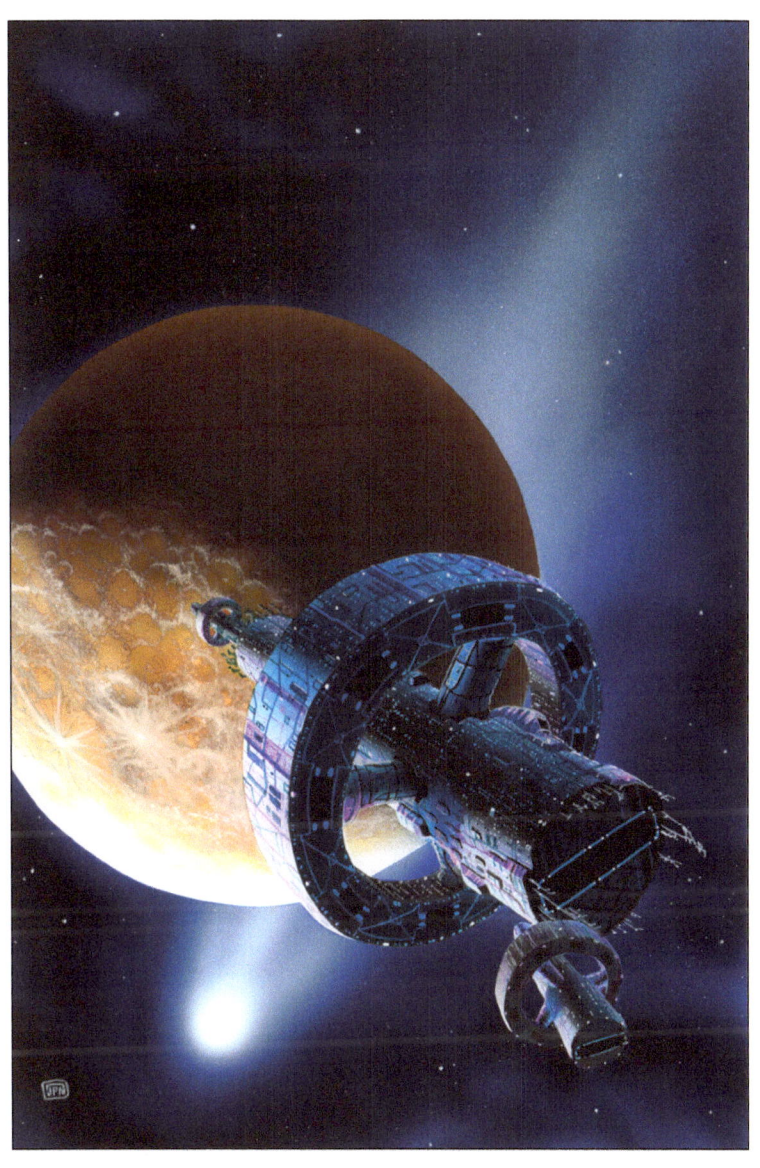

Borak

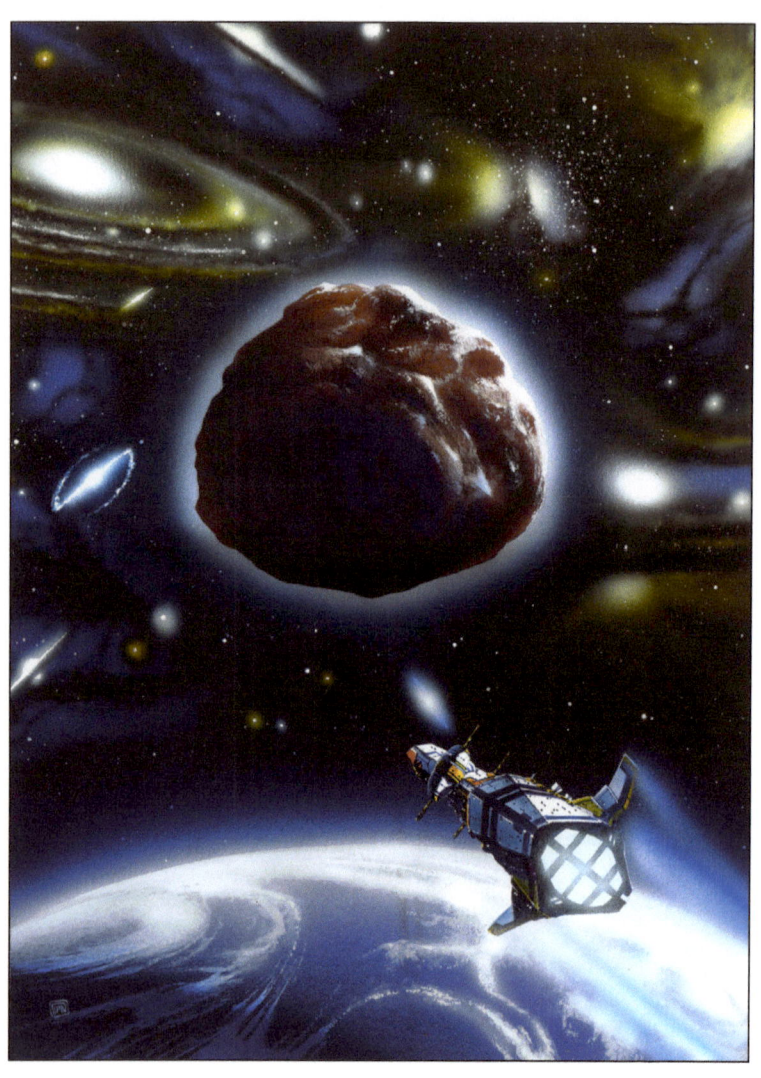

Eon

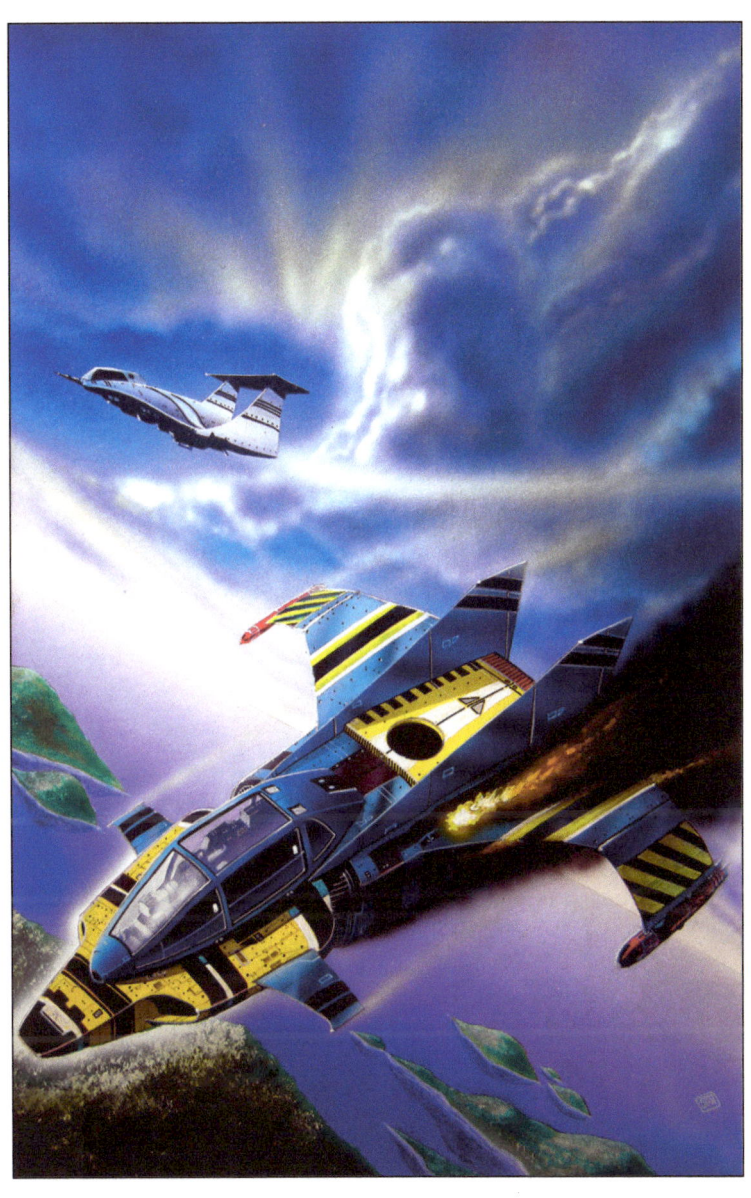

Sky of Flume

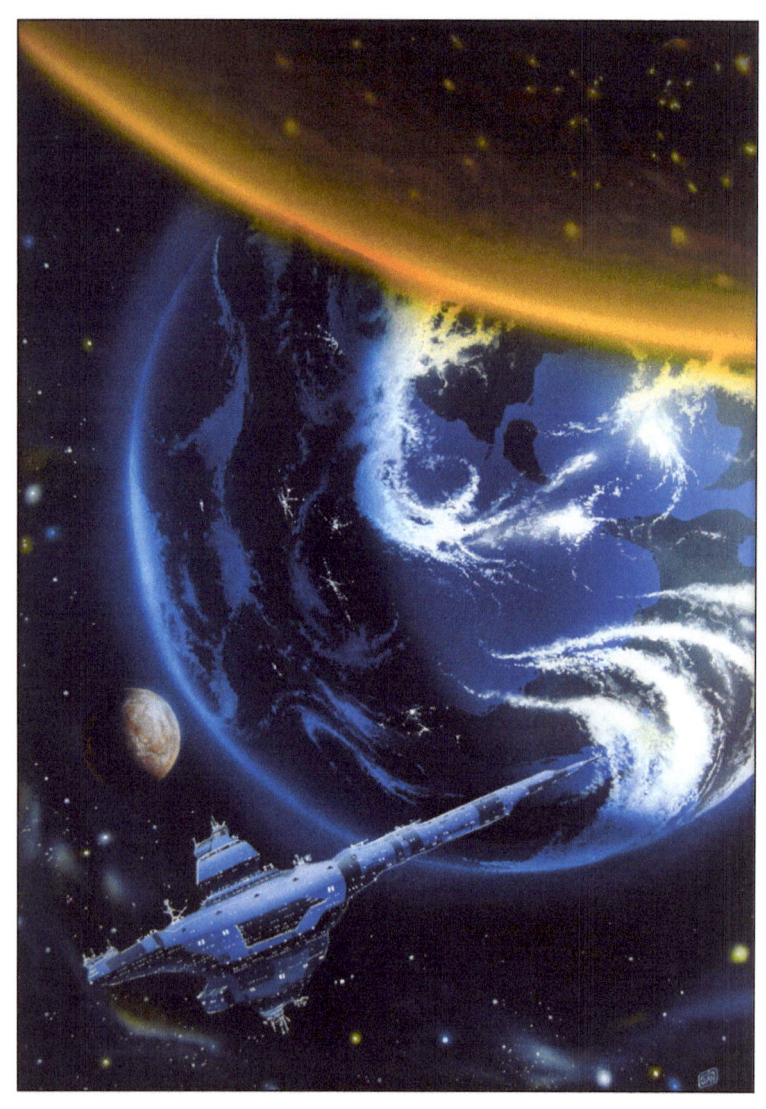

The Gate

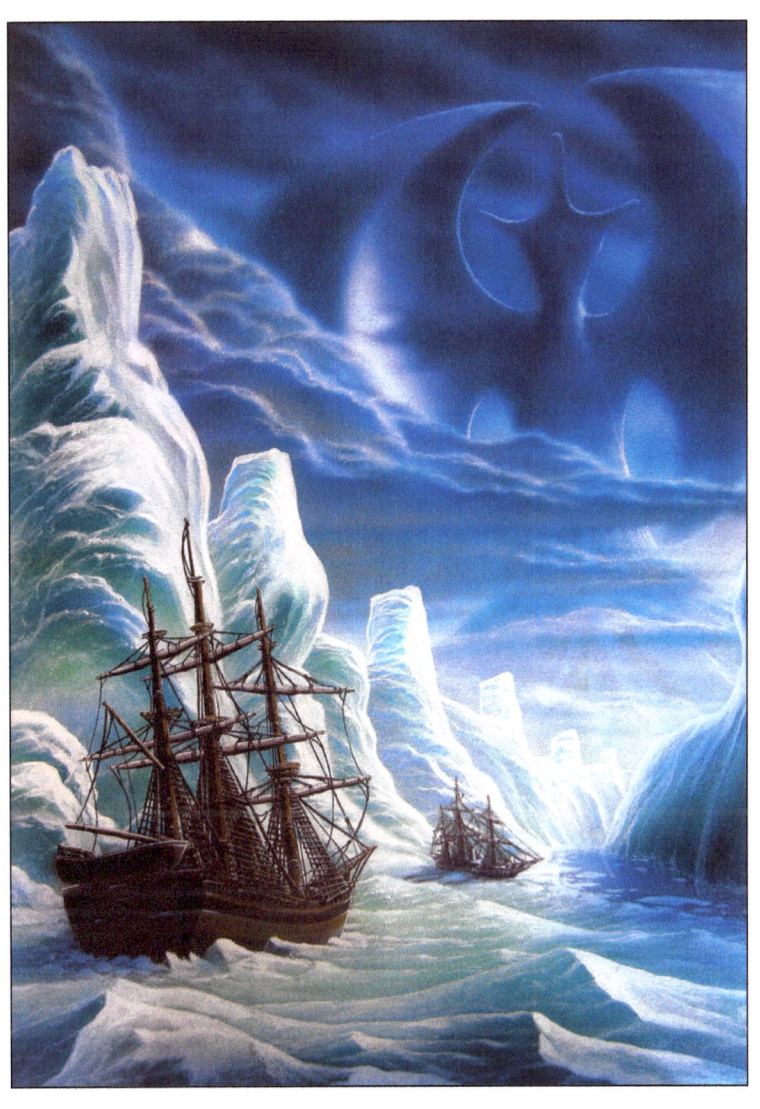

At the Mountains of Madness

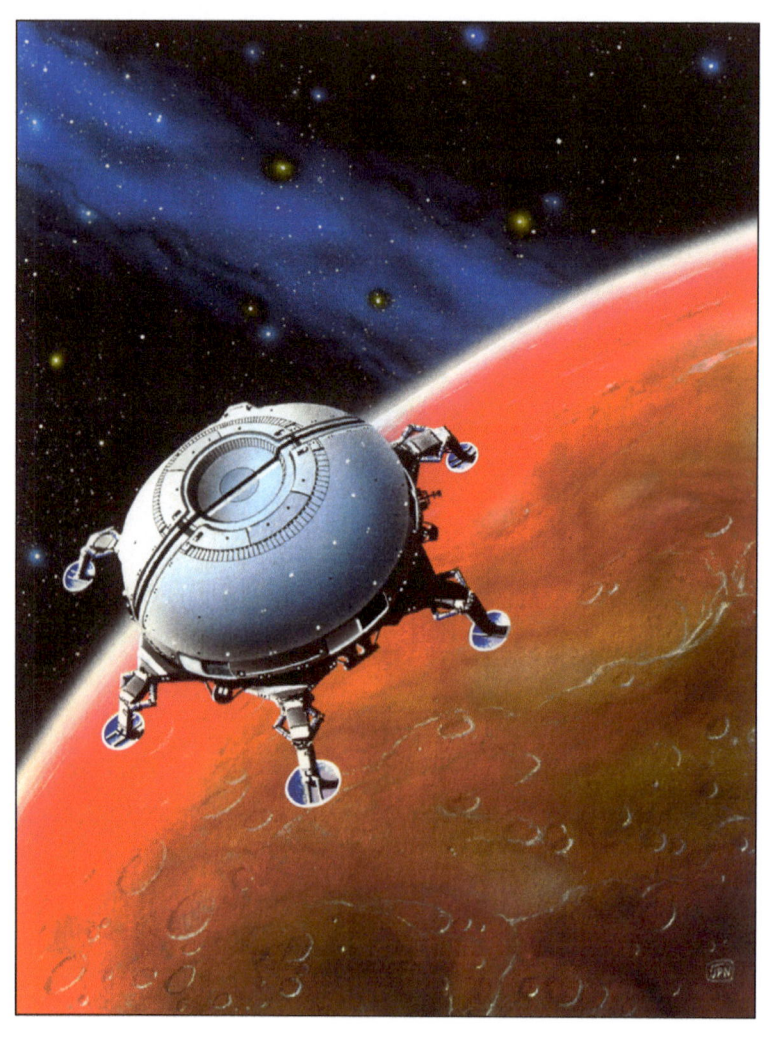

Penelope

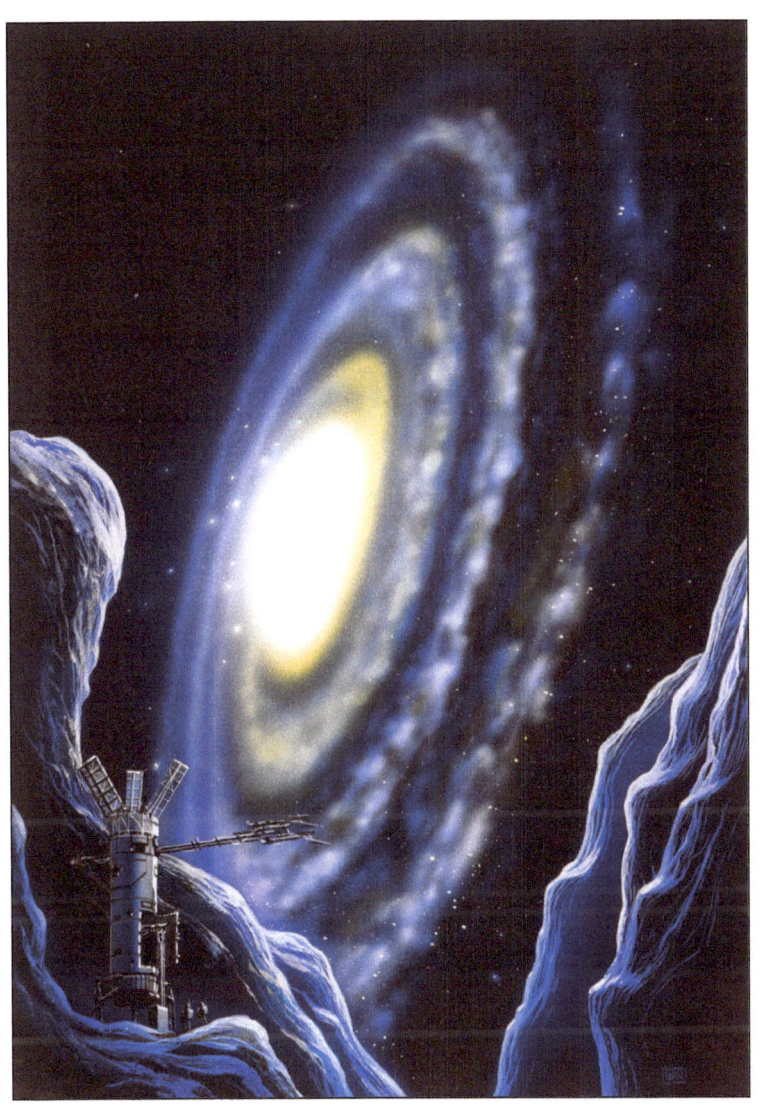

Galaxy

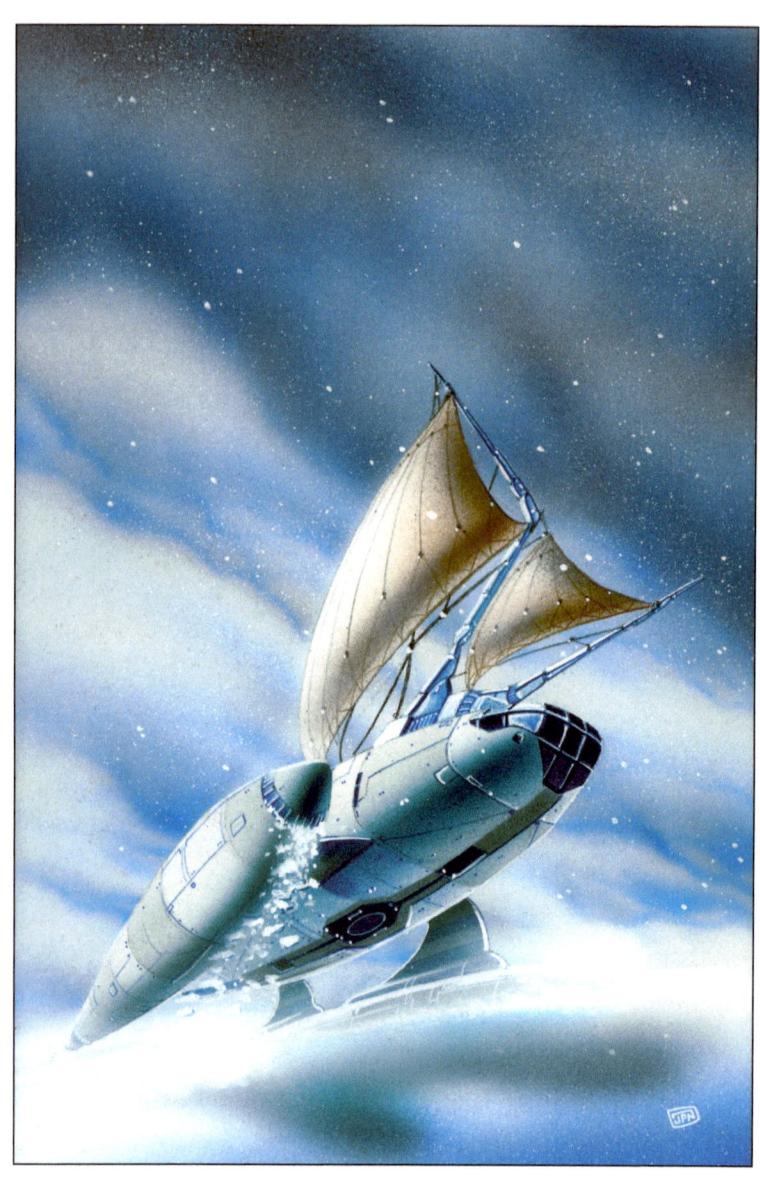

Phoenix

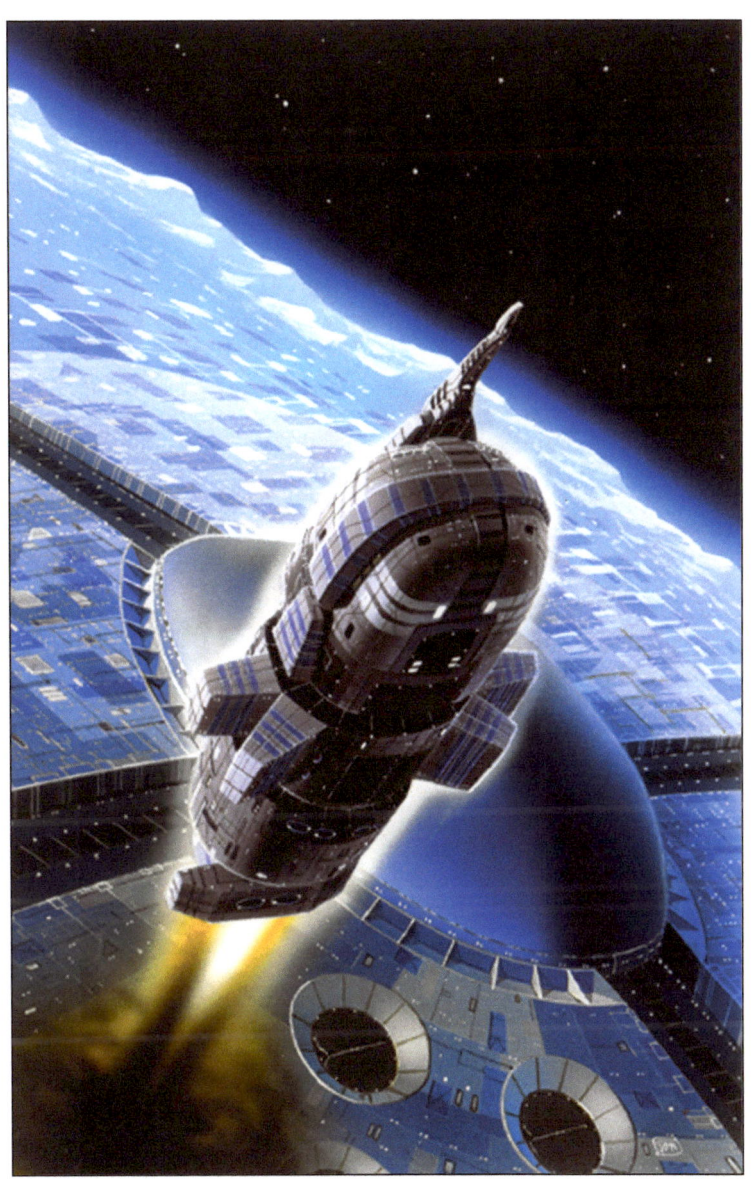

Colony 2

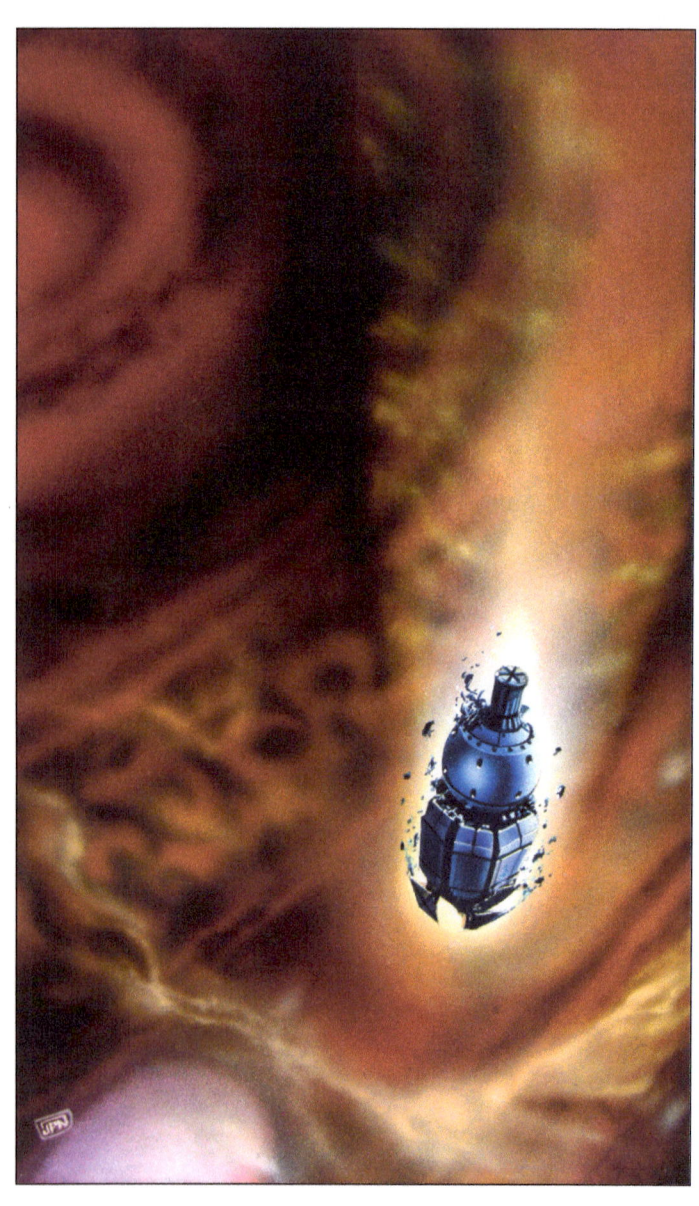

Meeting with Medusa 1

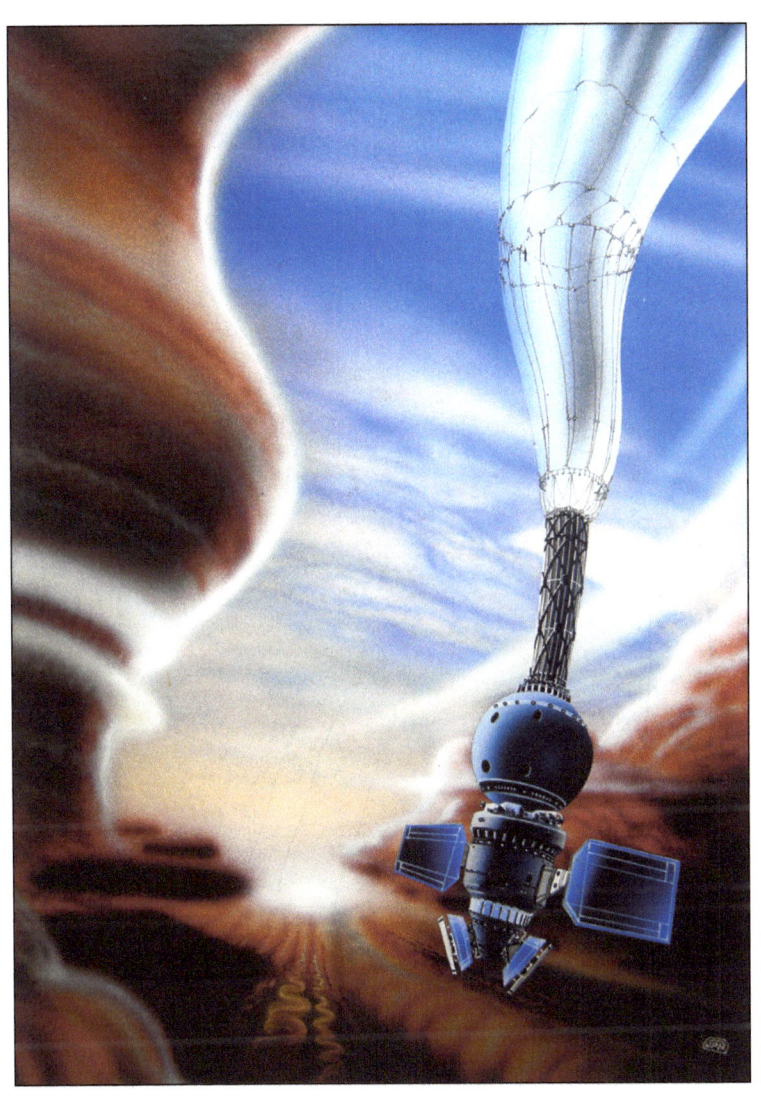

Meeting with Medusa 2

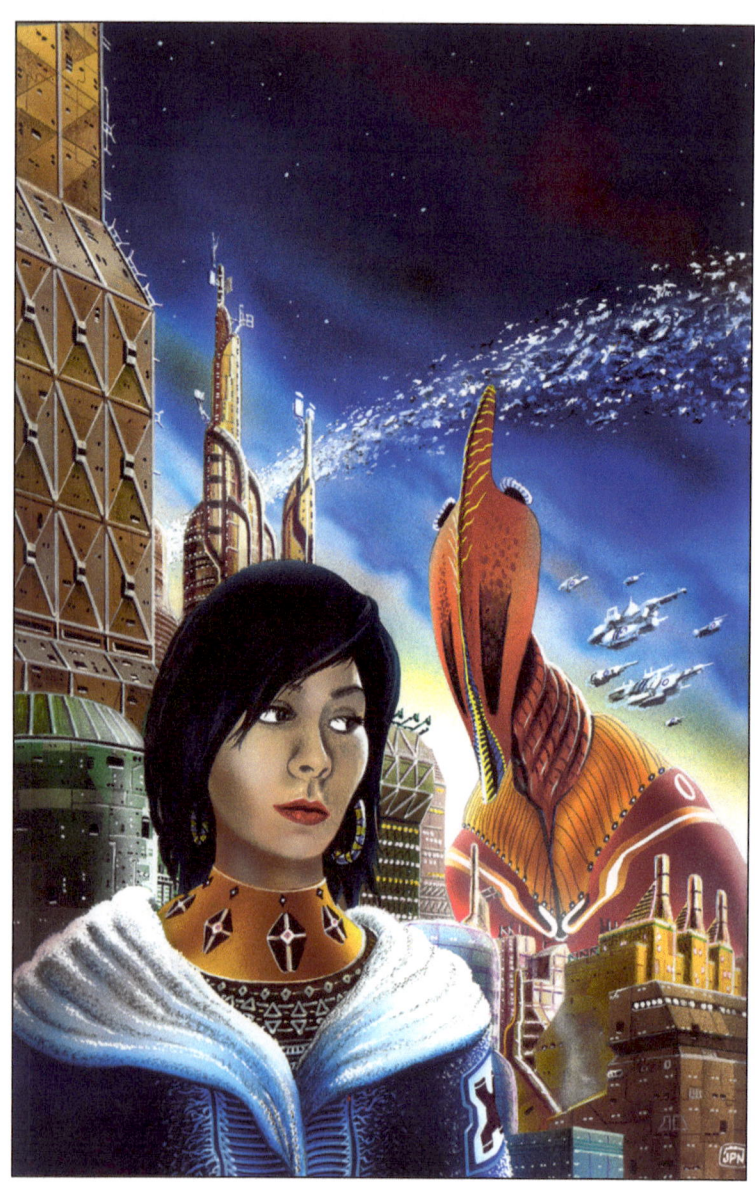

Solidarity

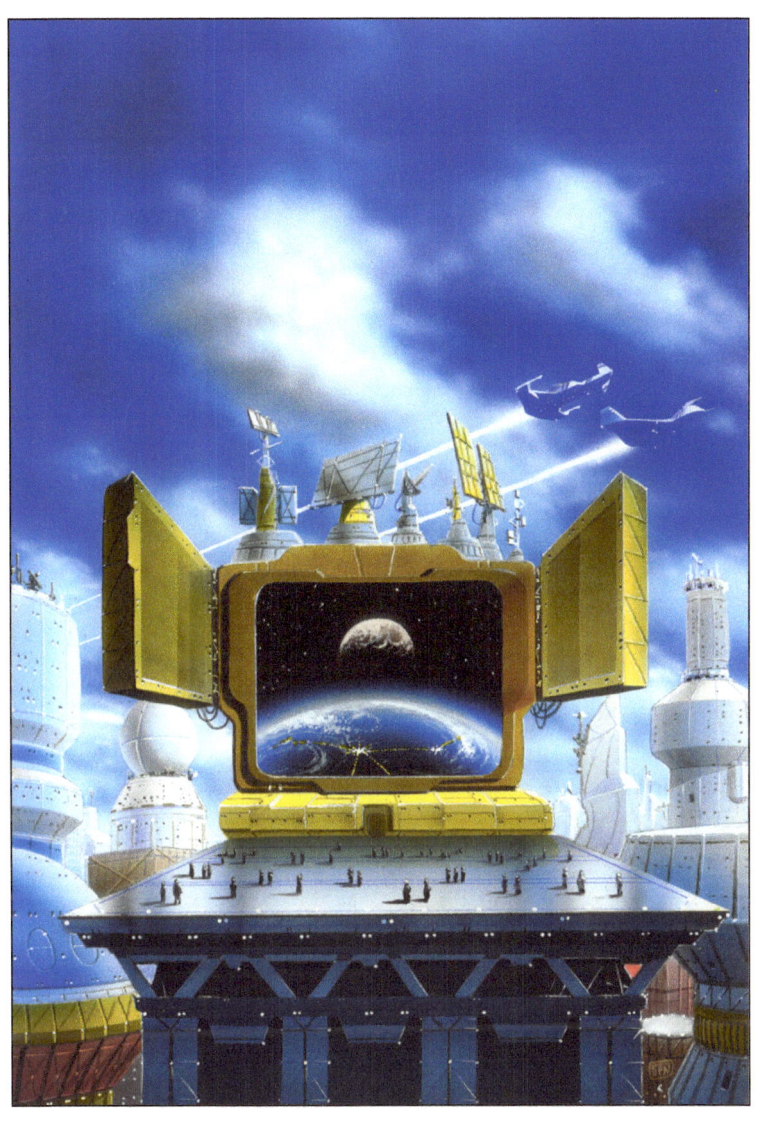

B2B

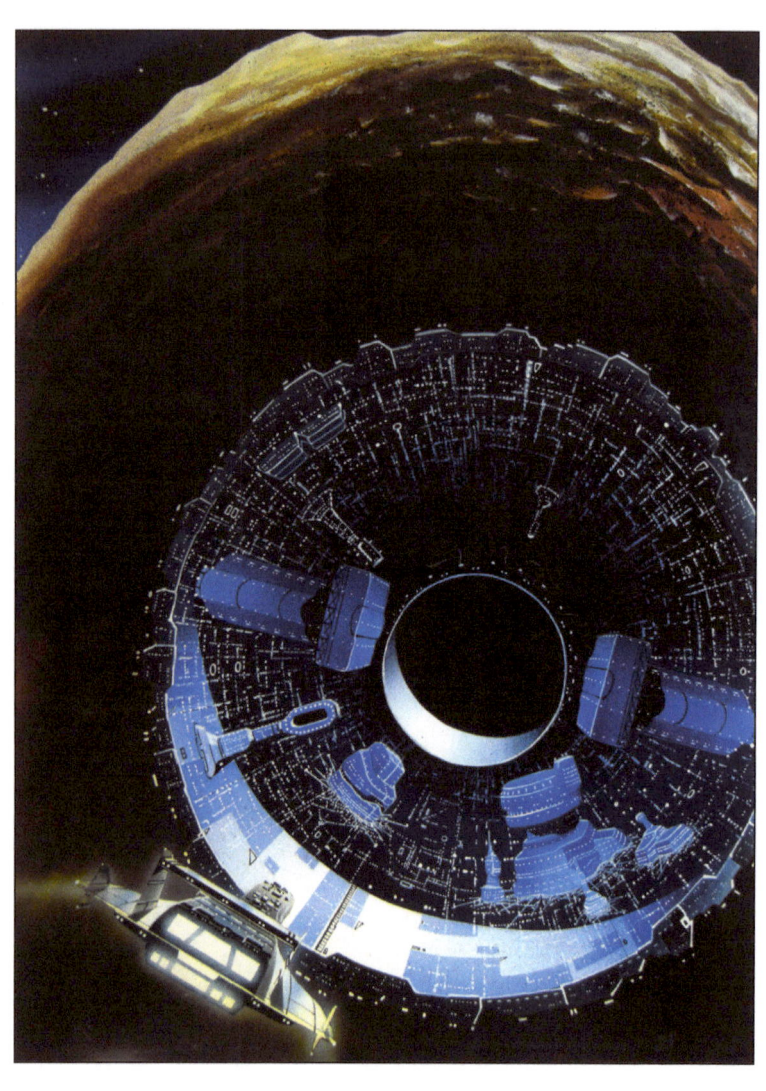

Asteroid Colony

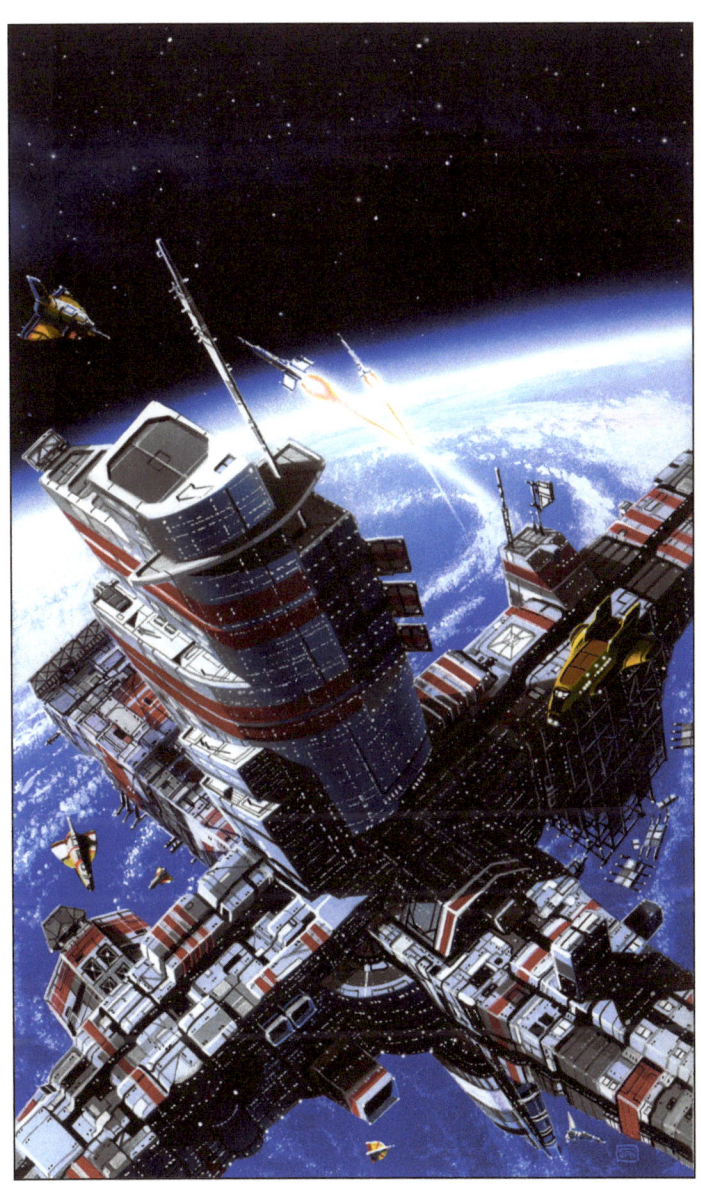

Space, Inc.

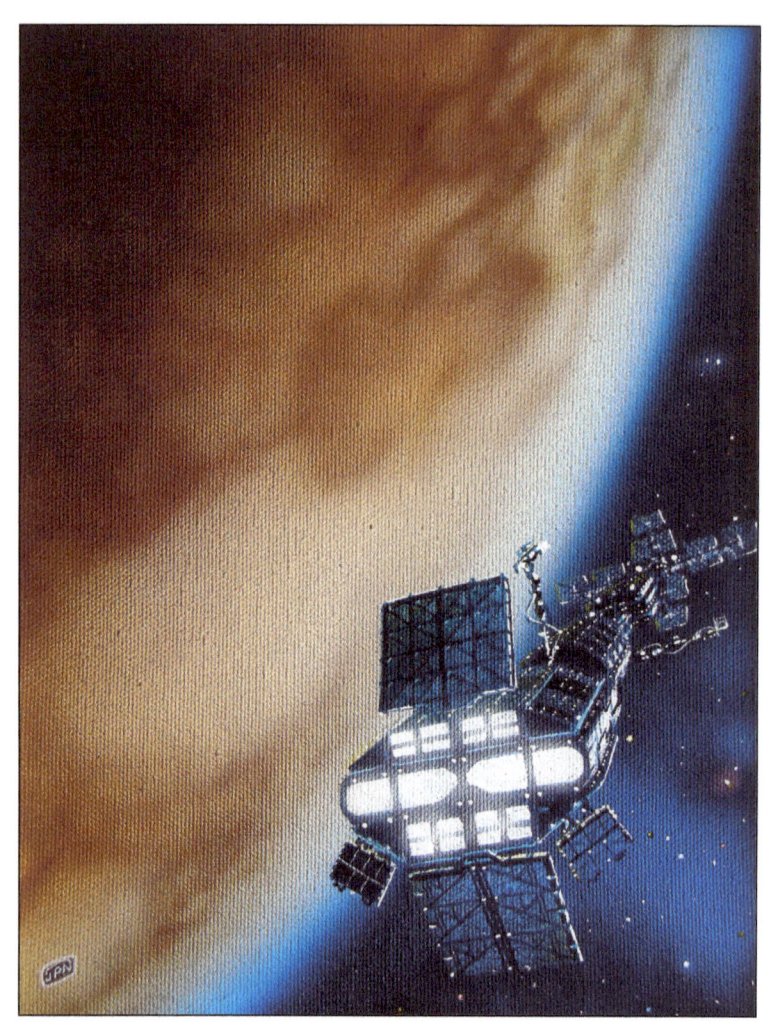

Orbit 6

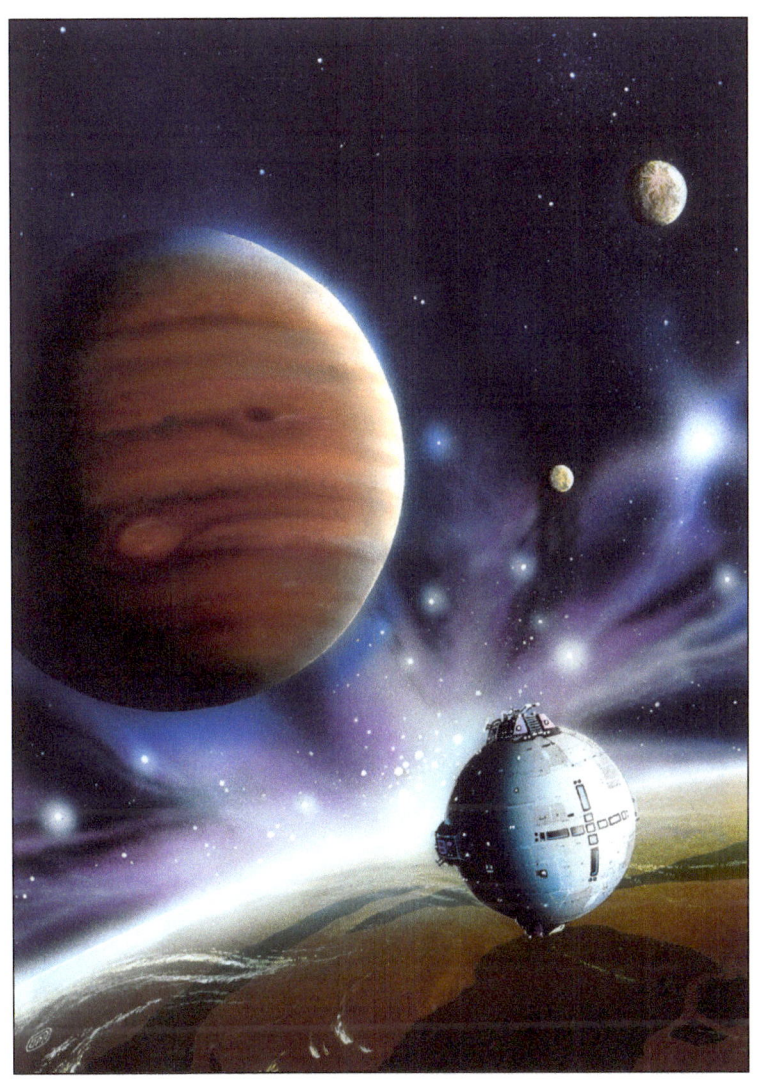

Orbit 8

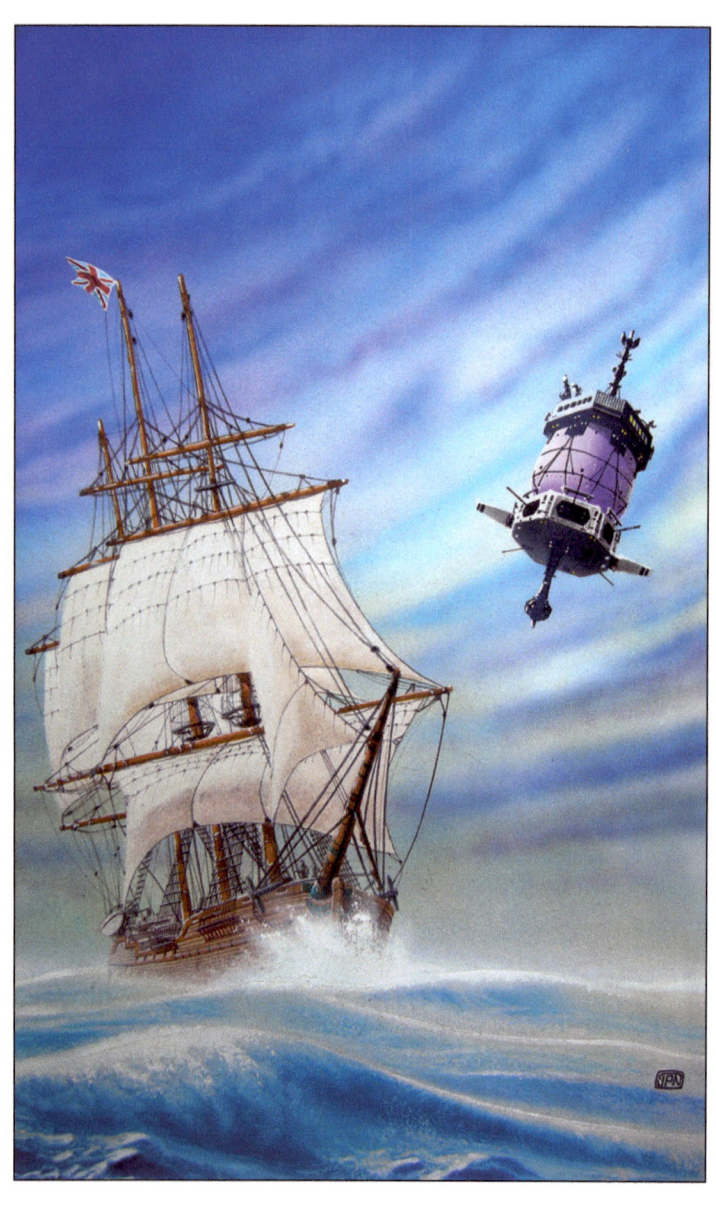

Timescape

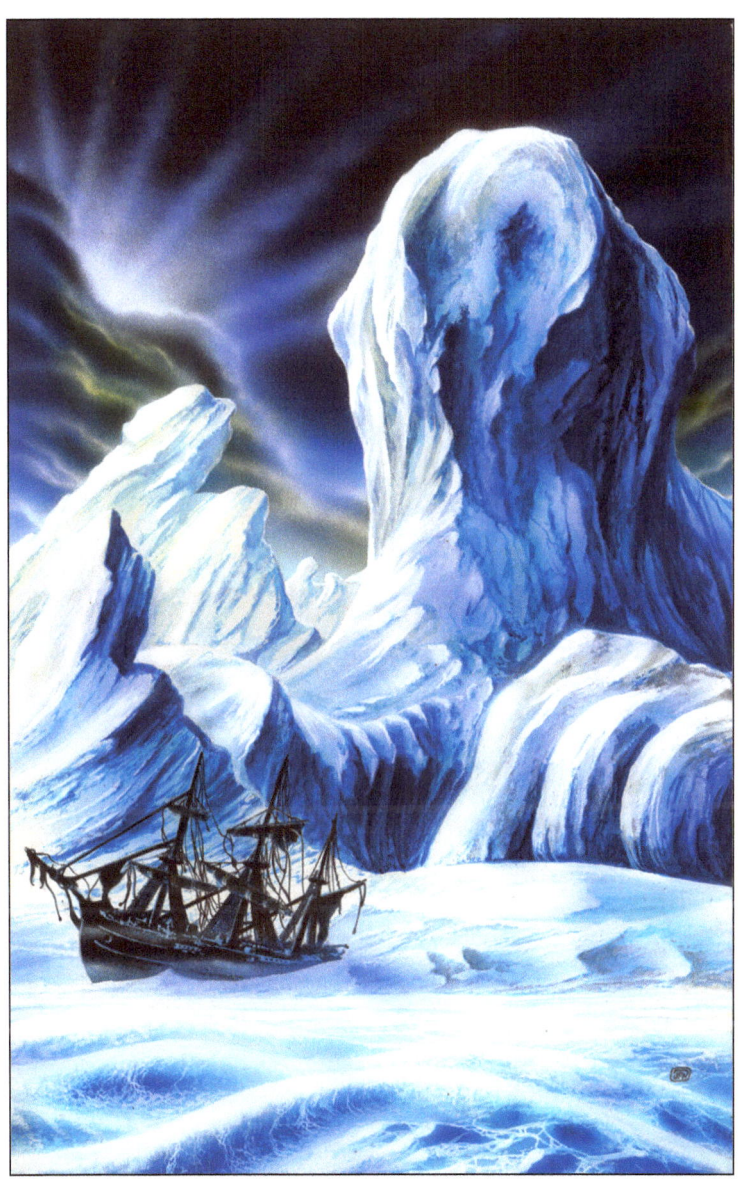

The Sphinx of the Ice

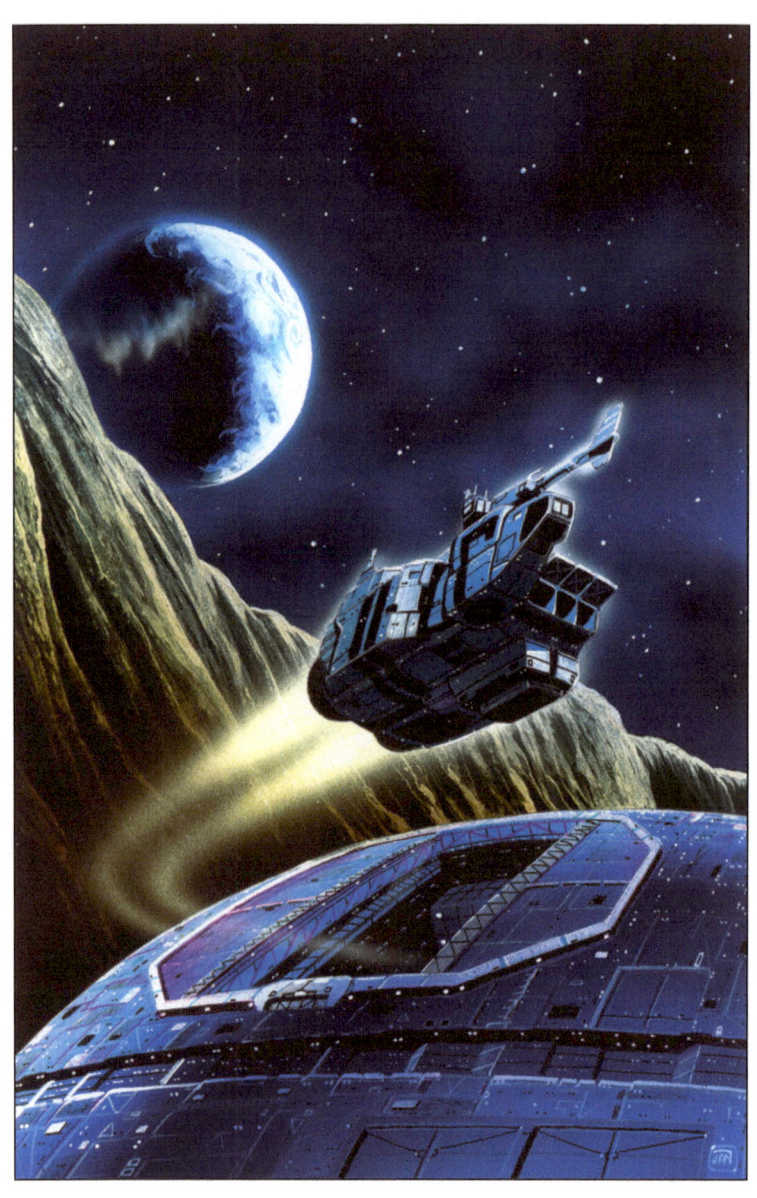

Above the Pole

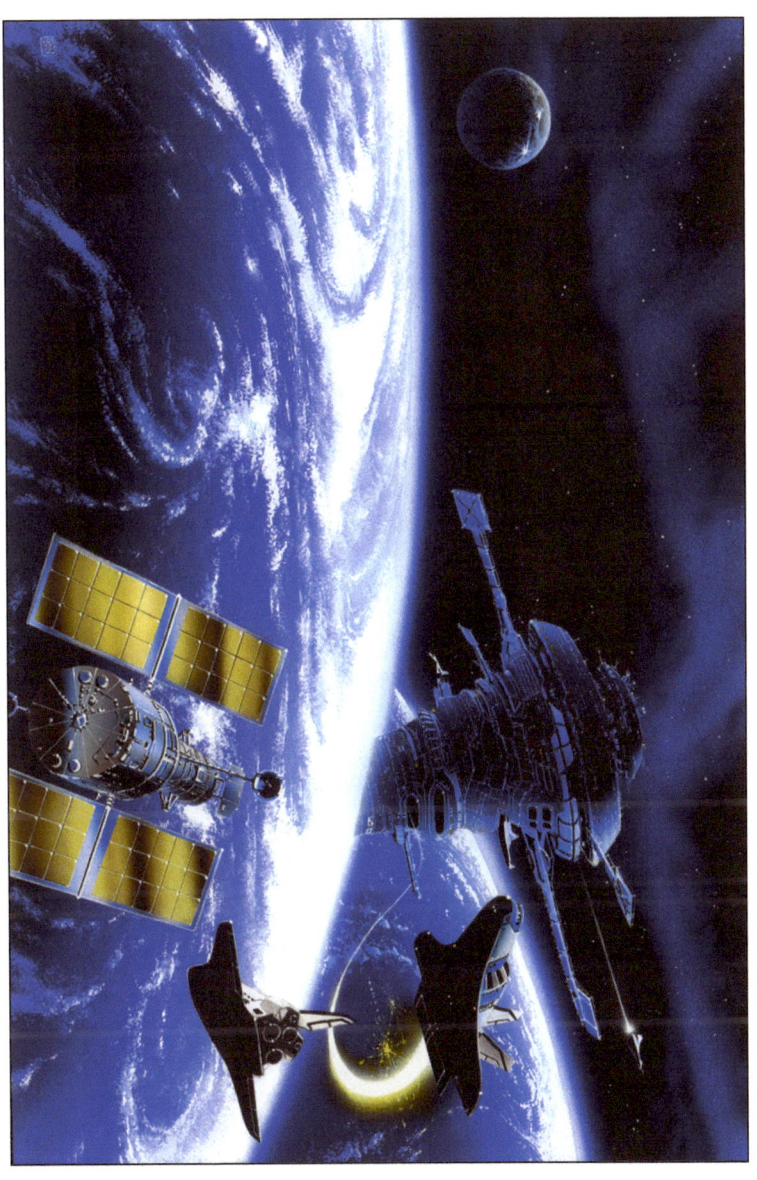

Orbiter

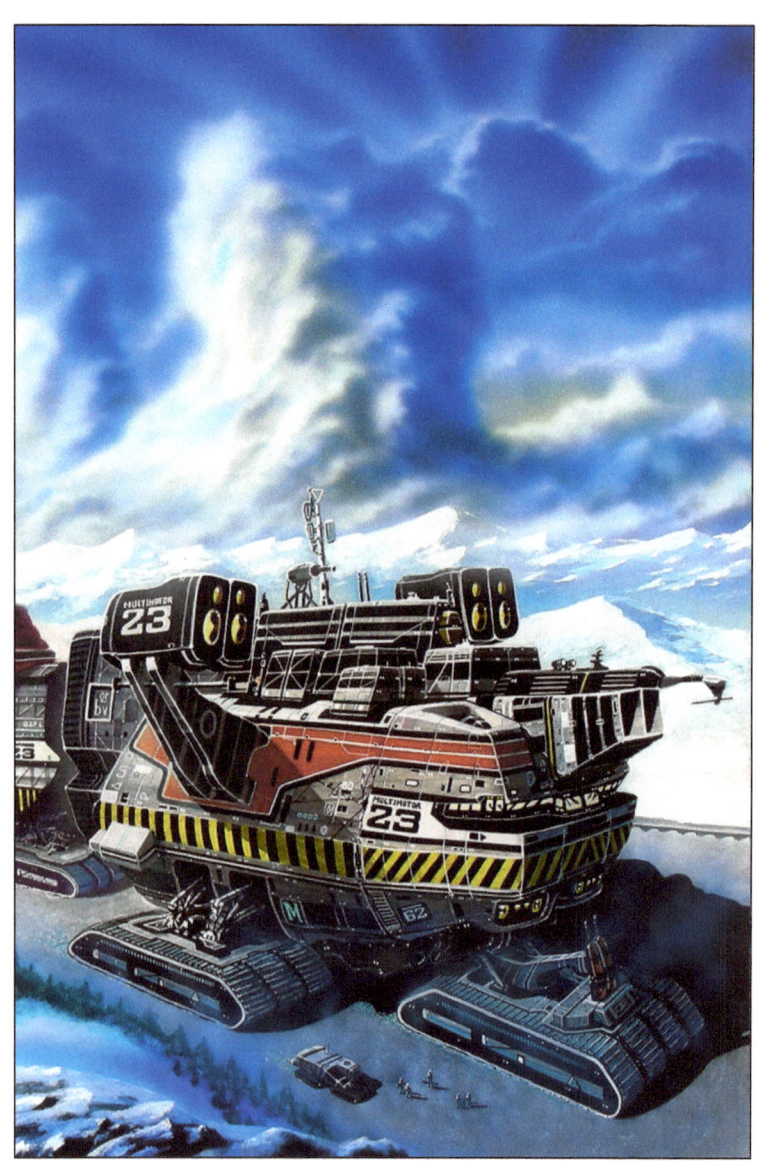

Electric North

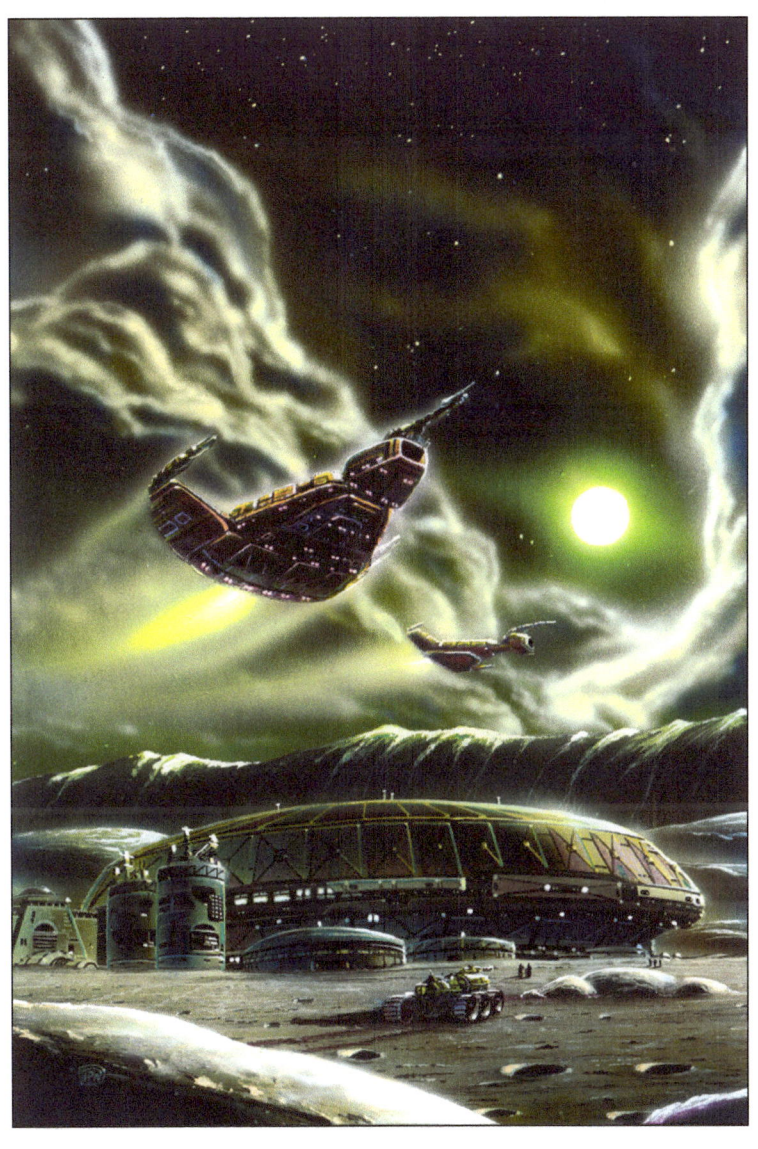

Moon Crater

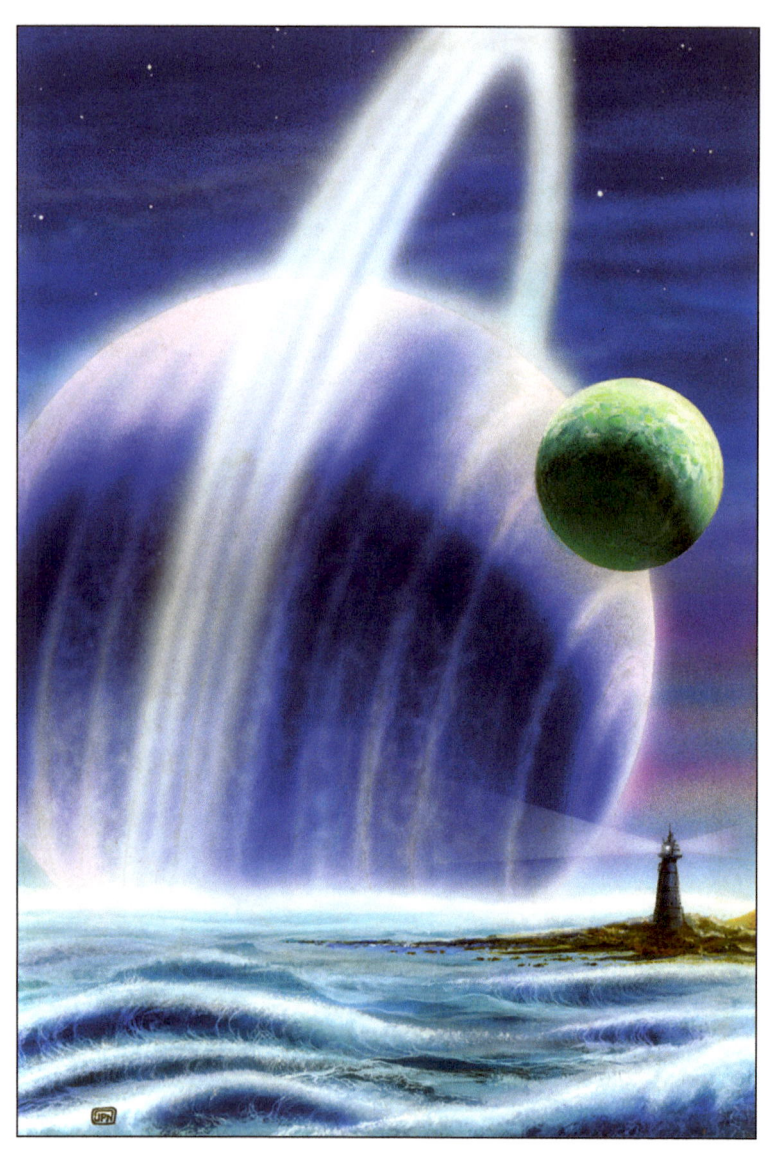

Lighthouse

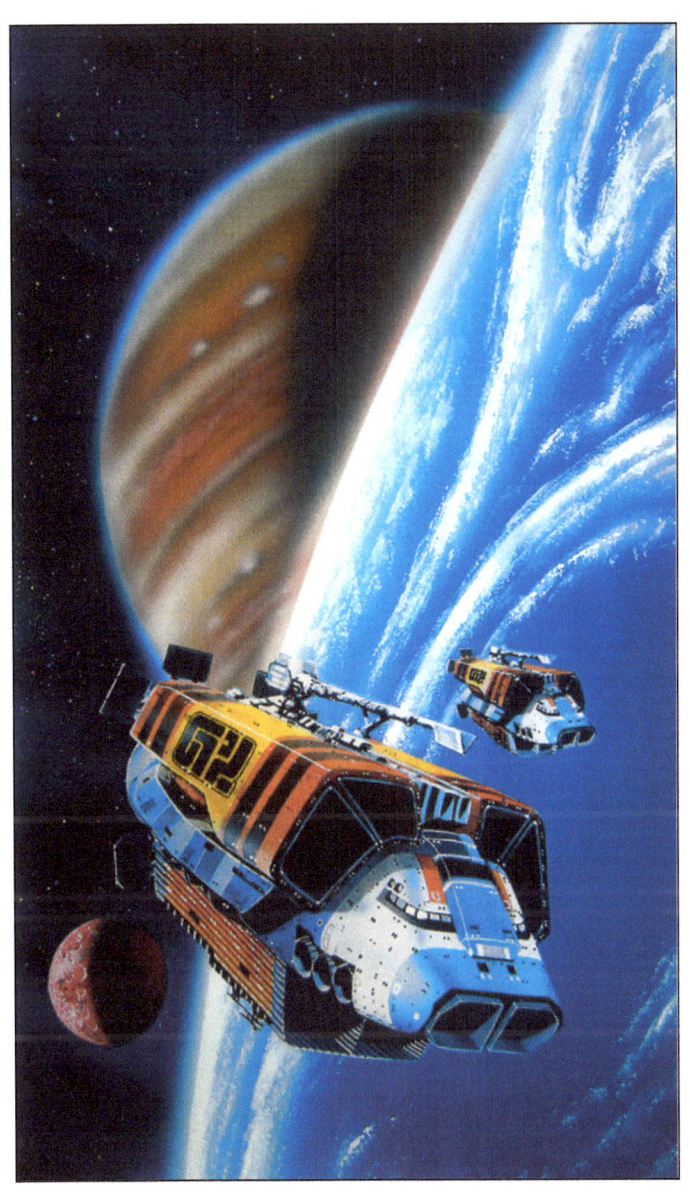

Cargo Ship

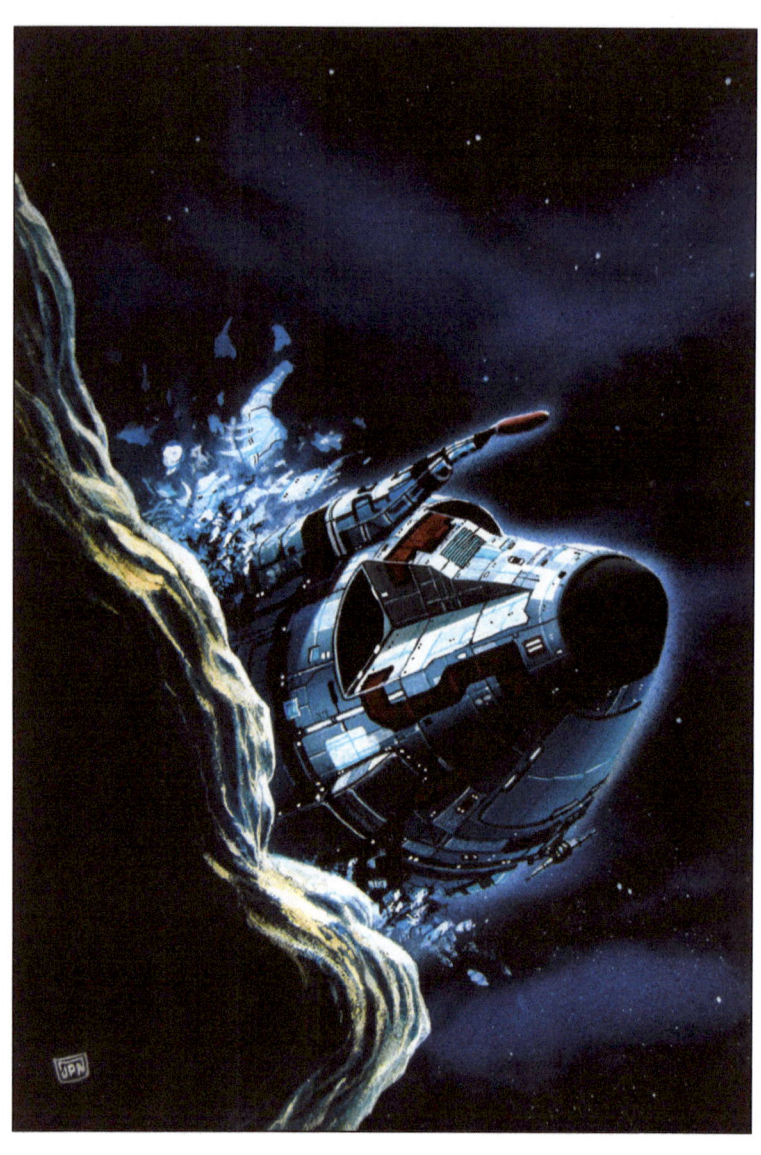

Collision

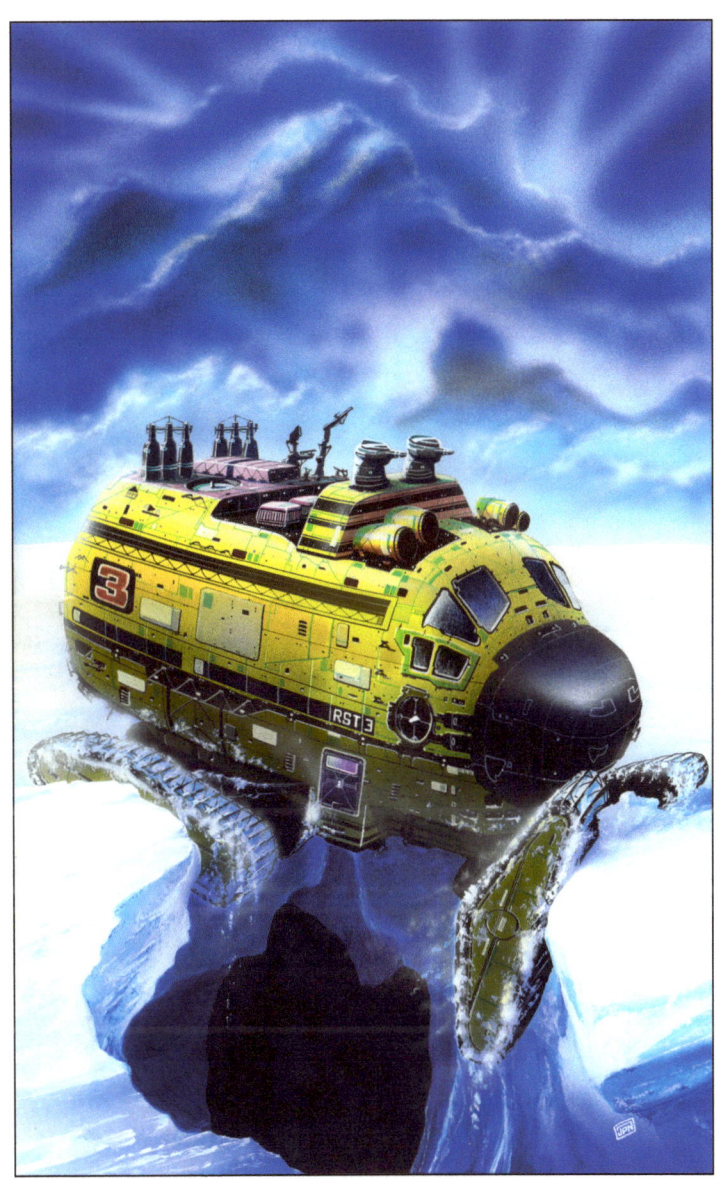

Polar Perils

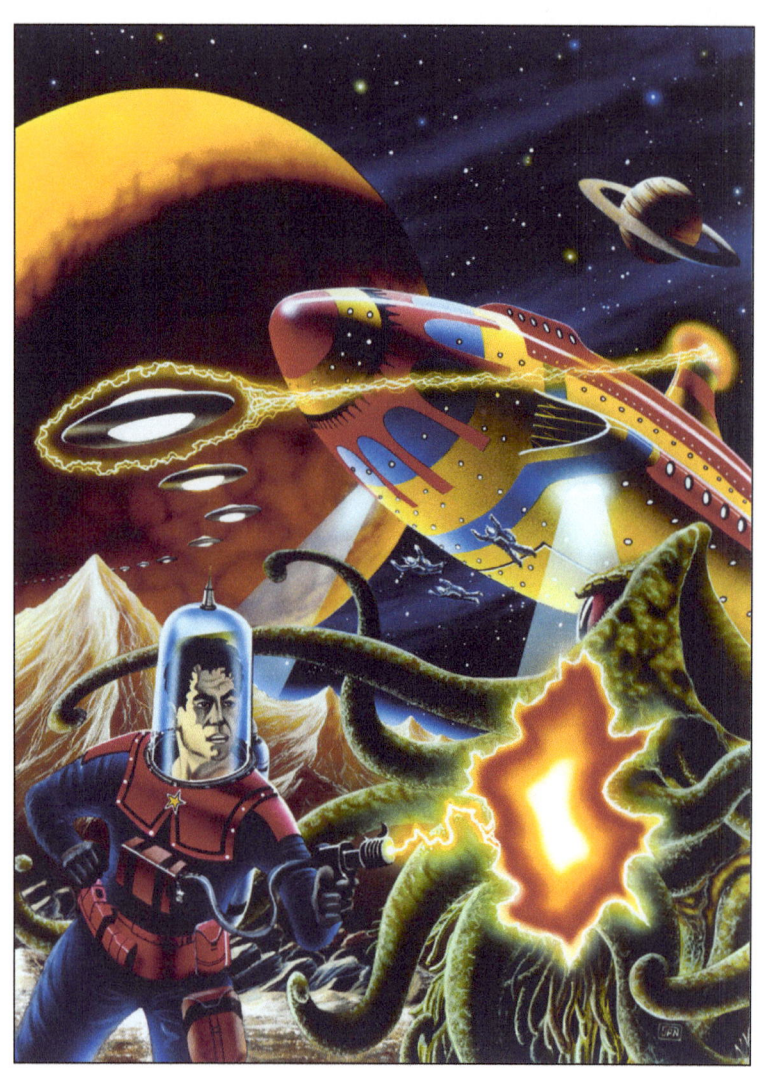

Pulp Action

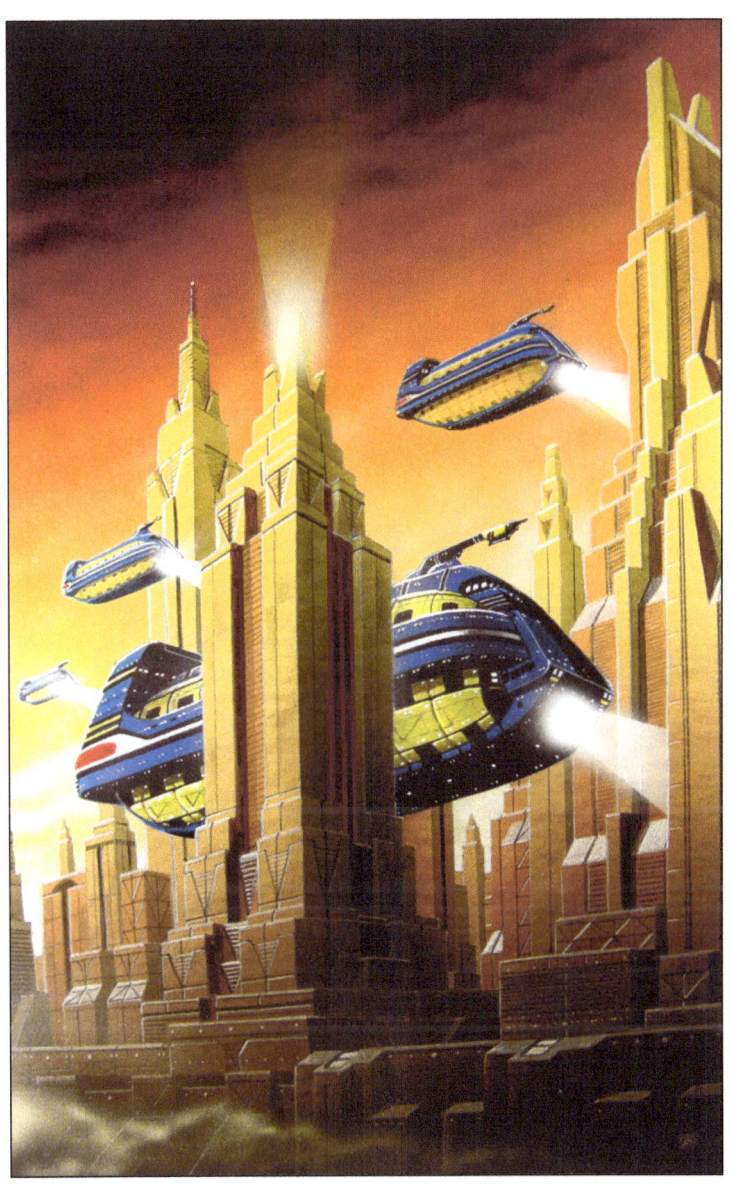

City

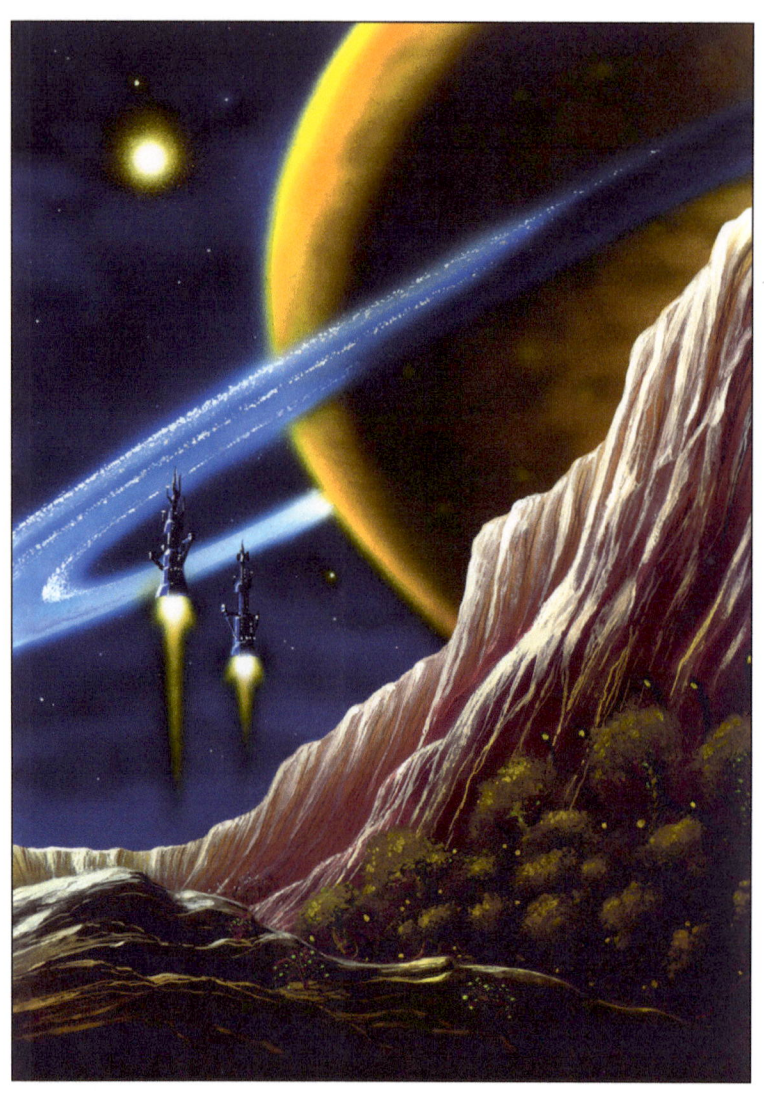

Open Space

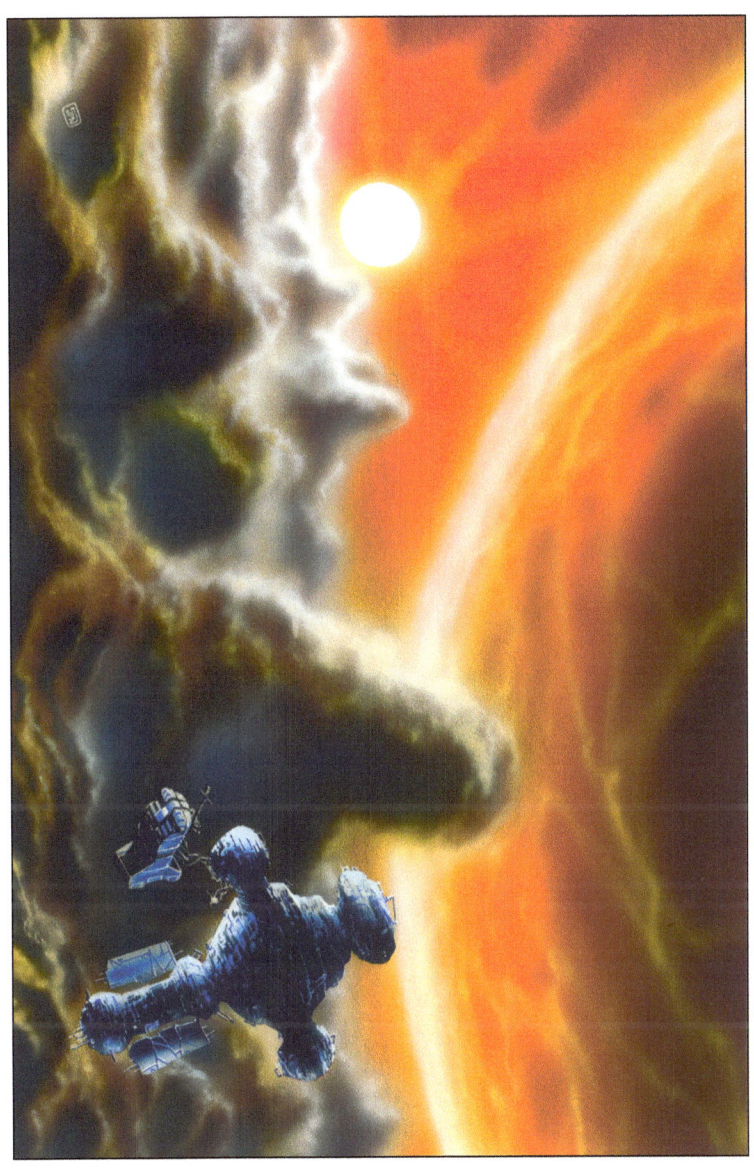

Floating Station

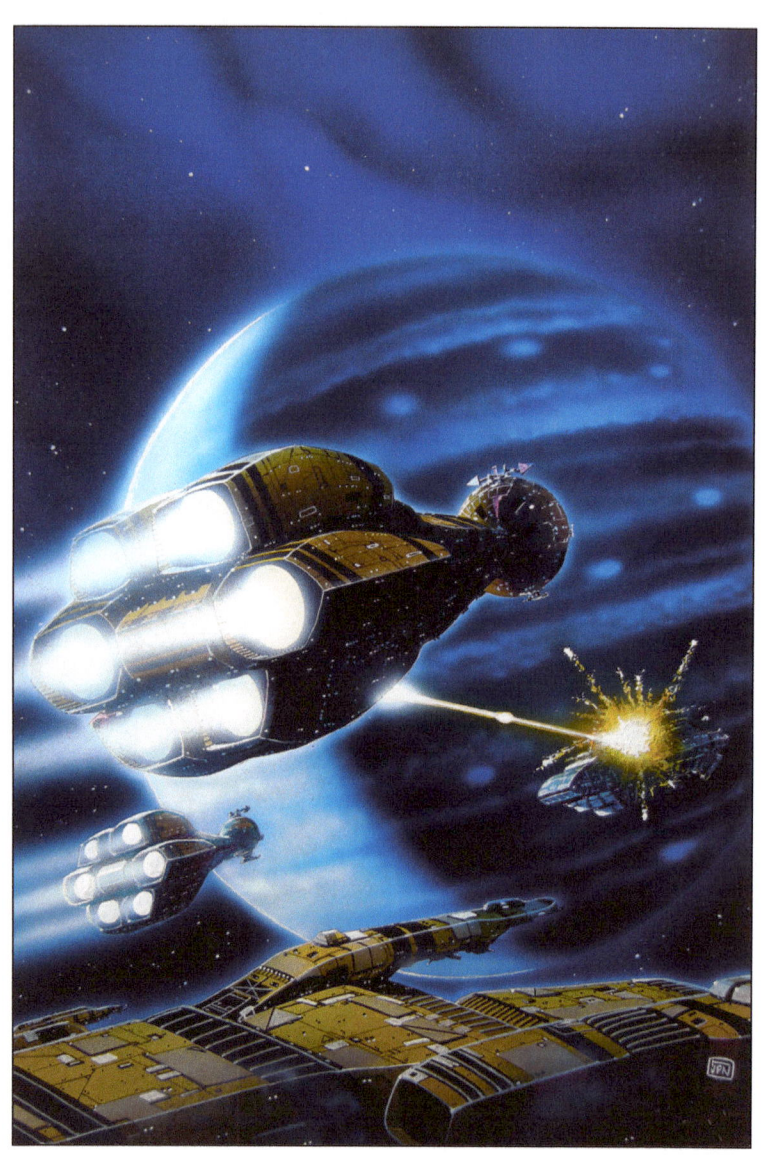

Space Opera

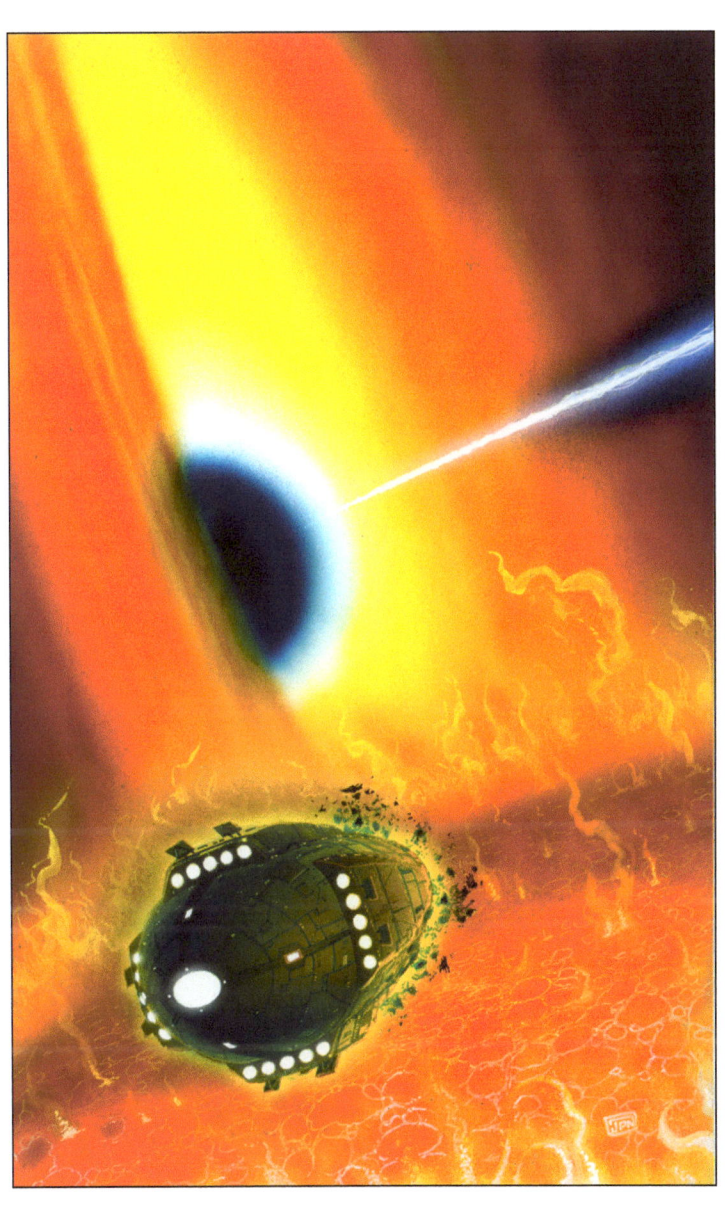

The Engine of Recall

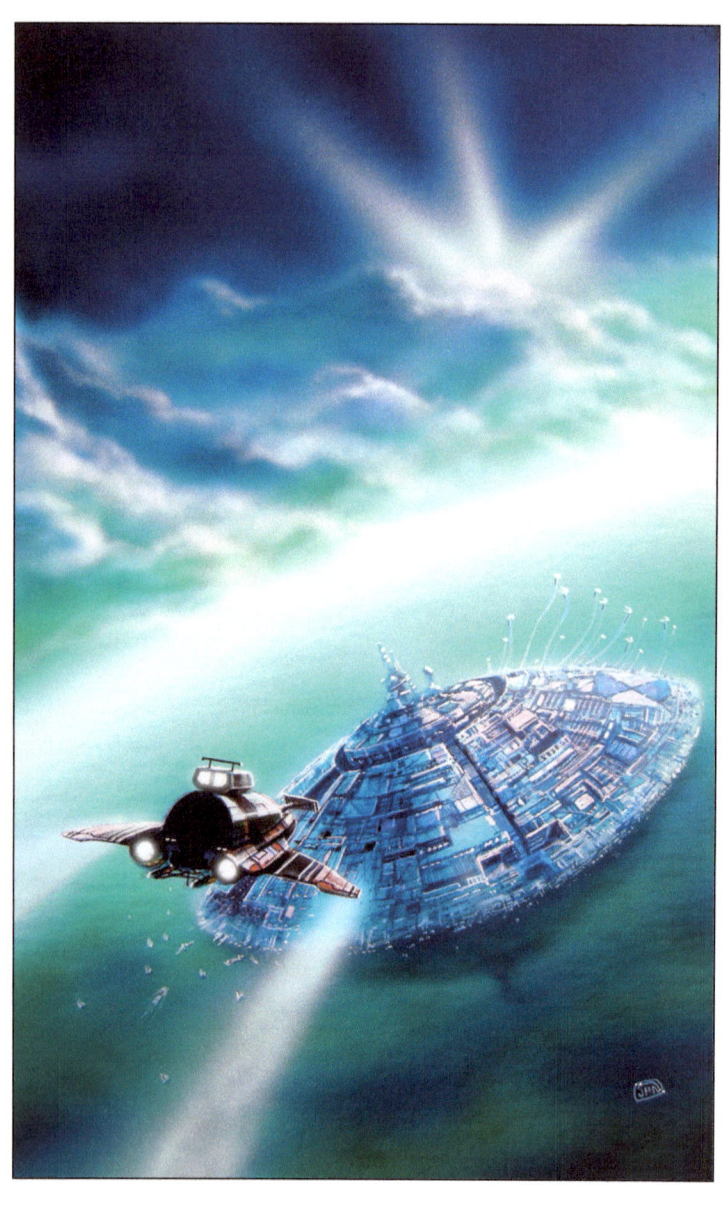

Floating City

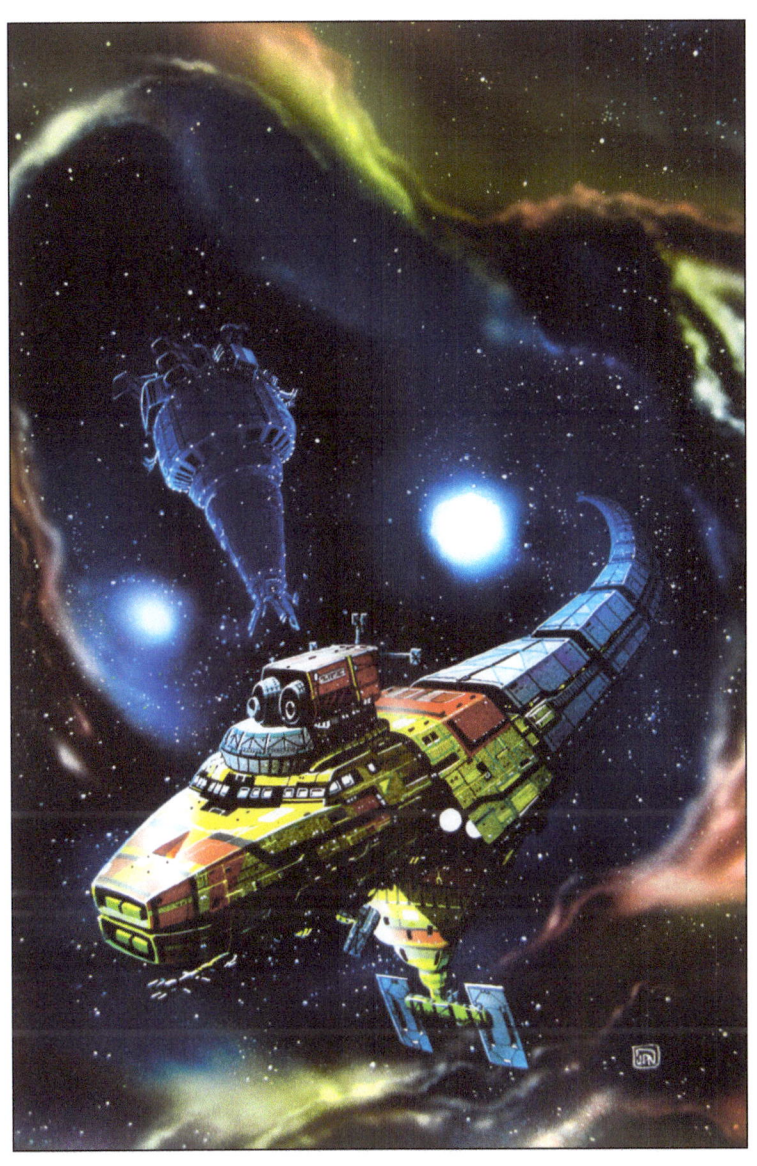

Wagon Train

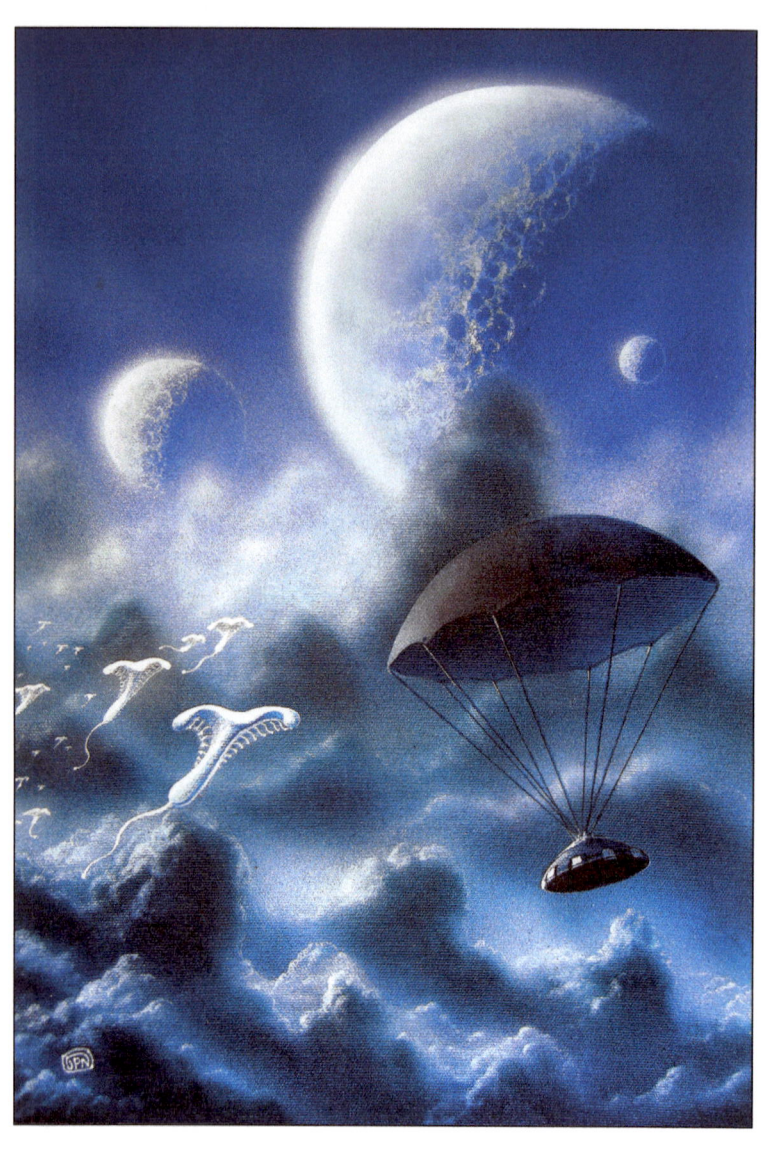

First Encounter

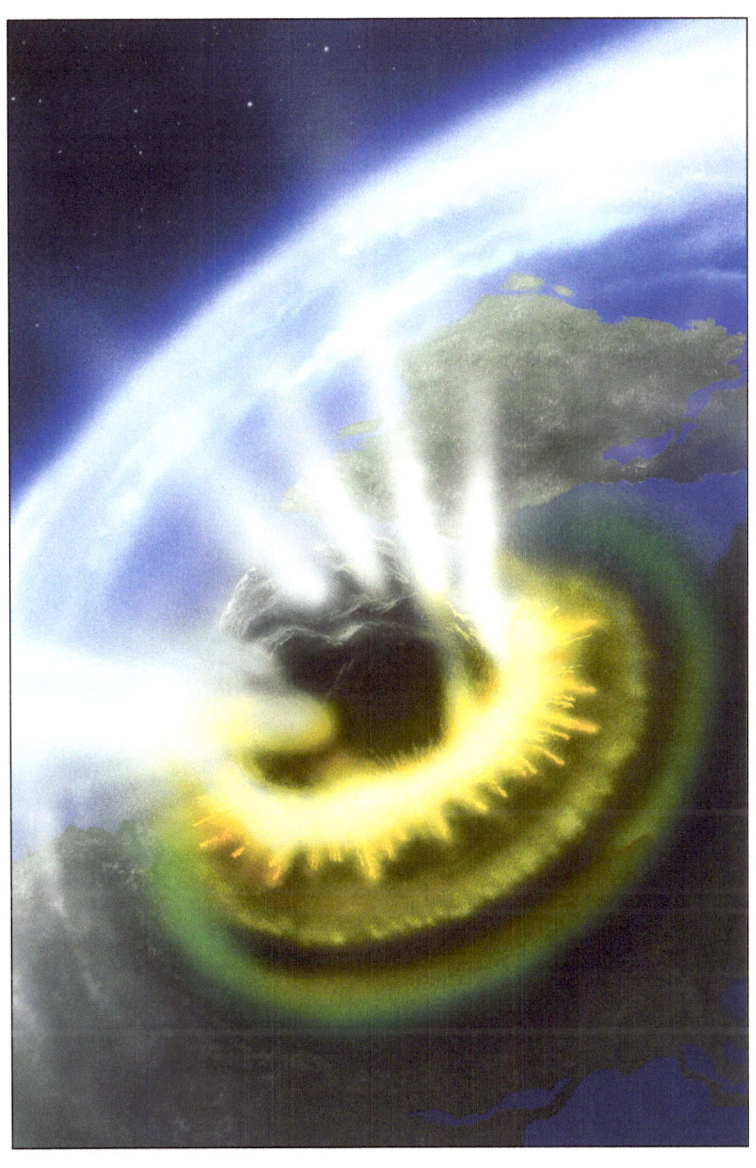

Impact

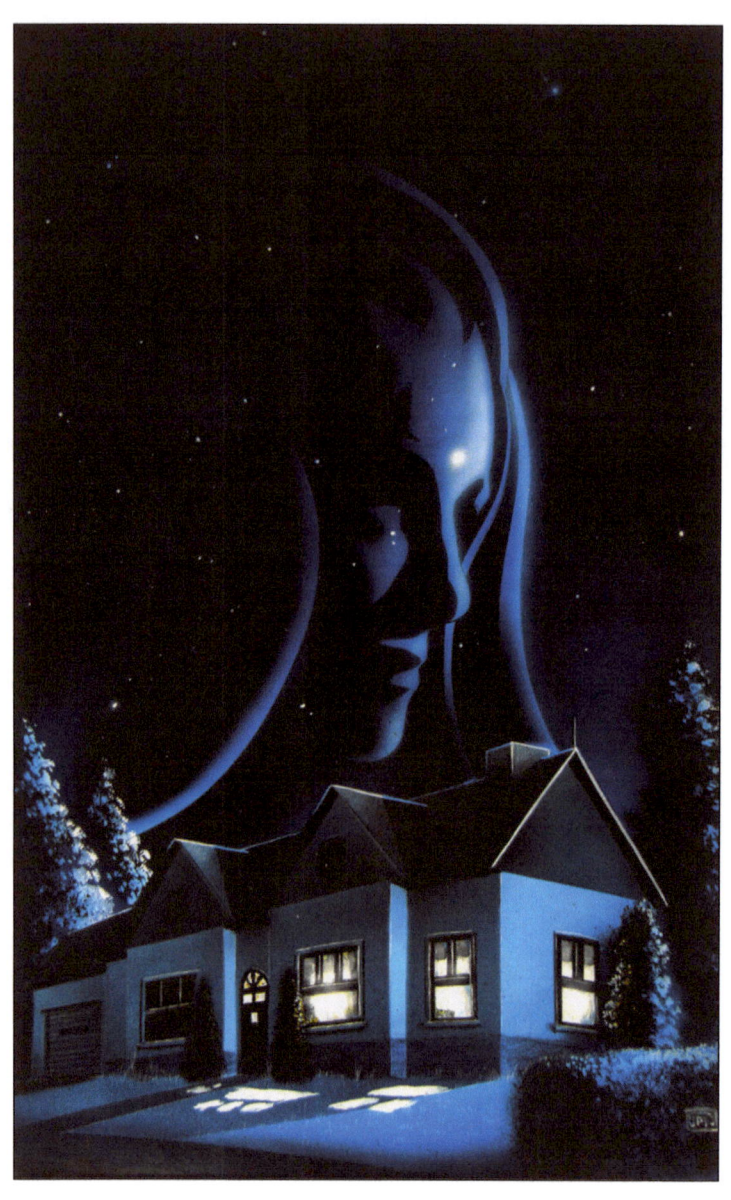

Ghost

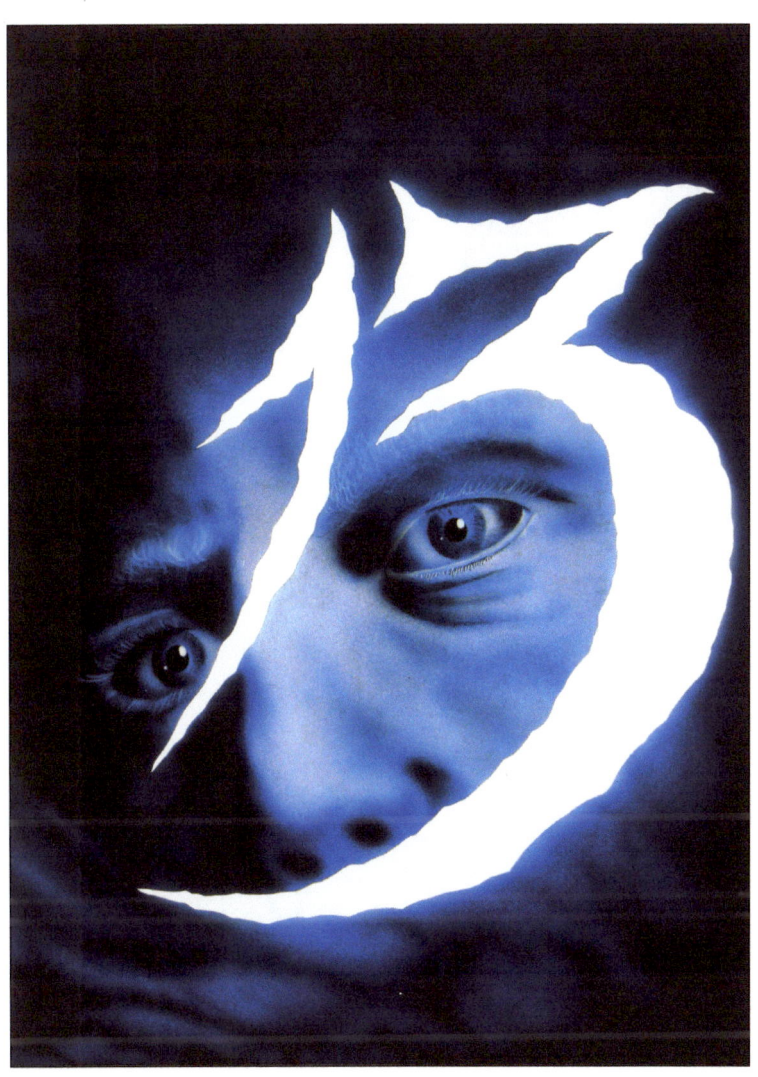

13

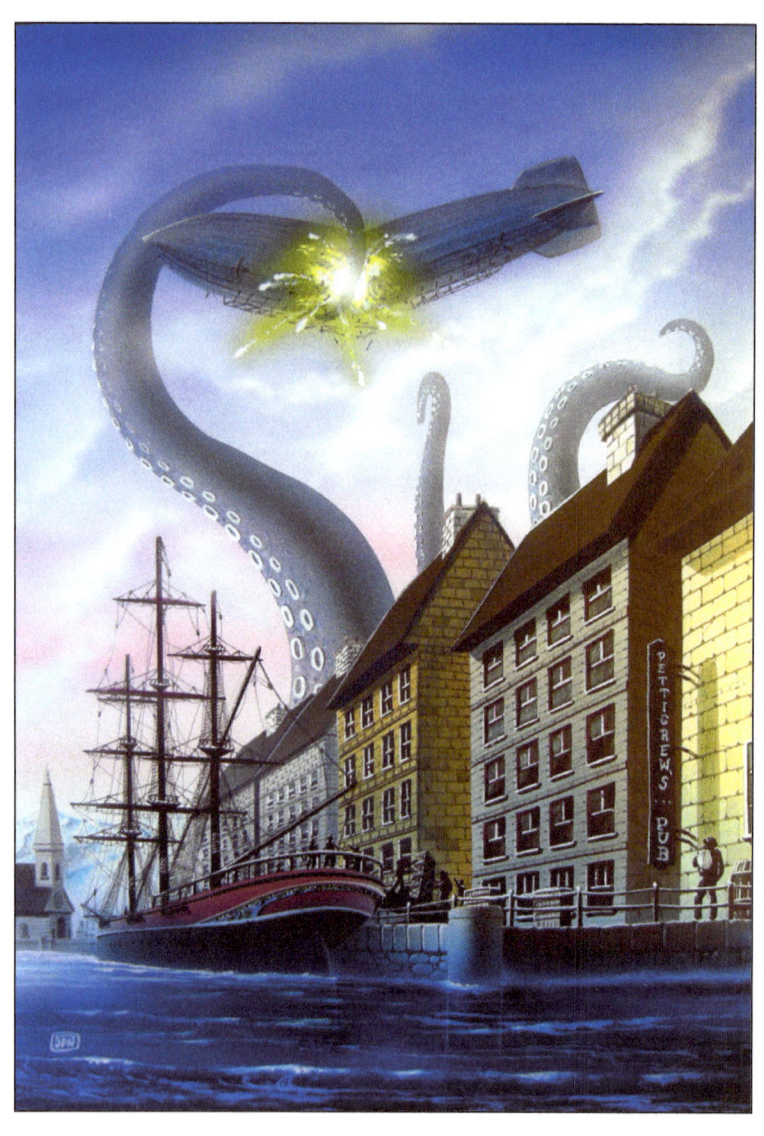

Old Port

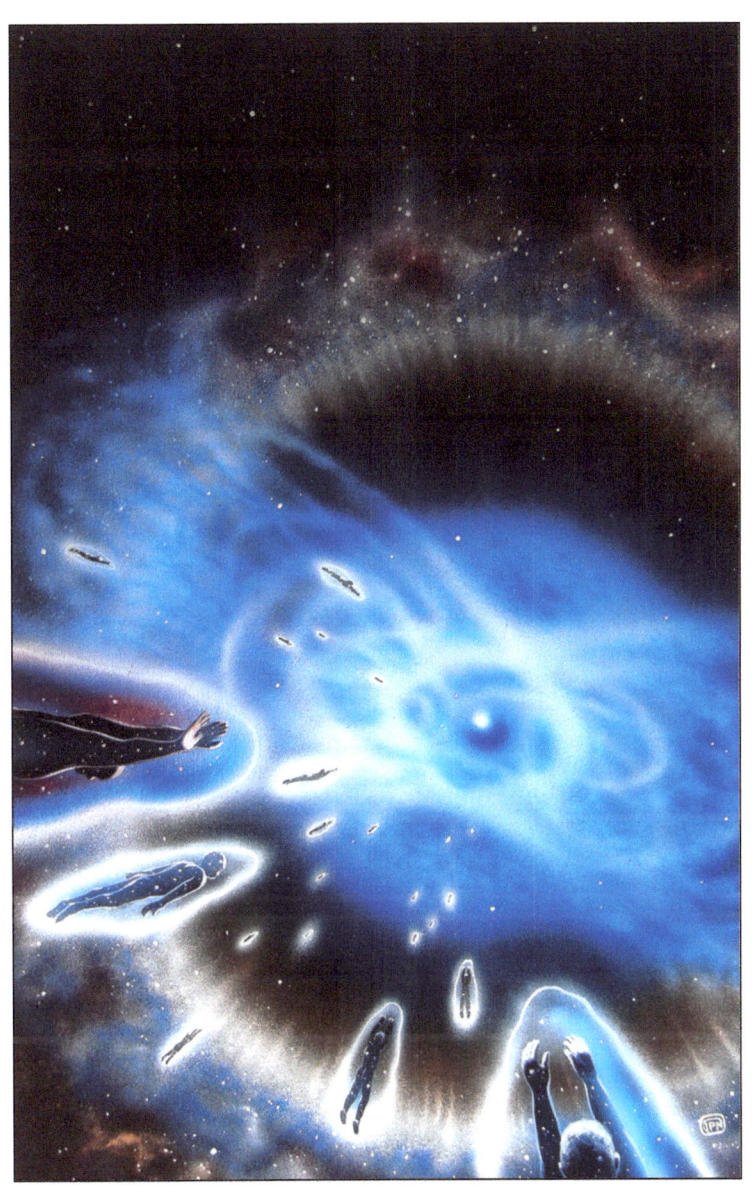

Icarus Beach

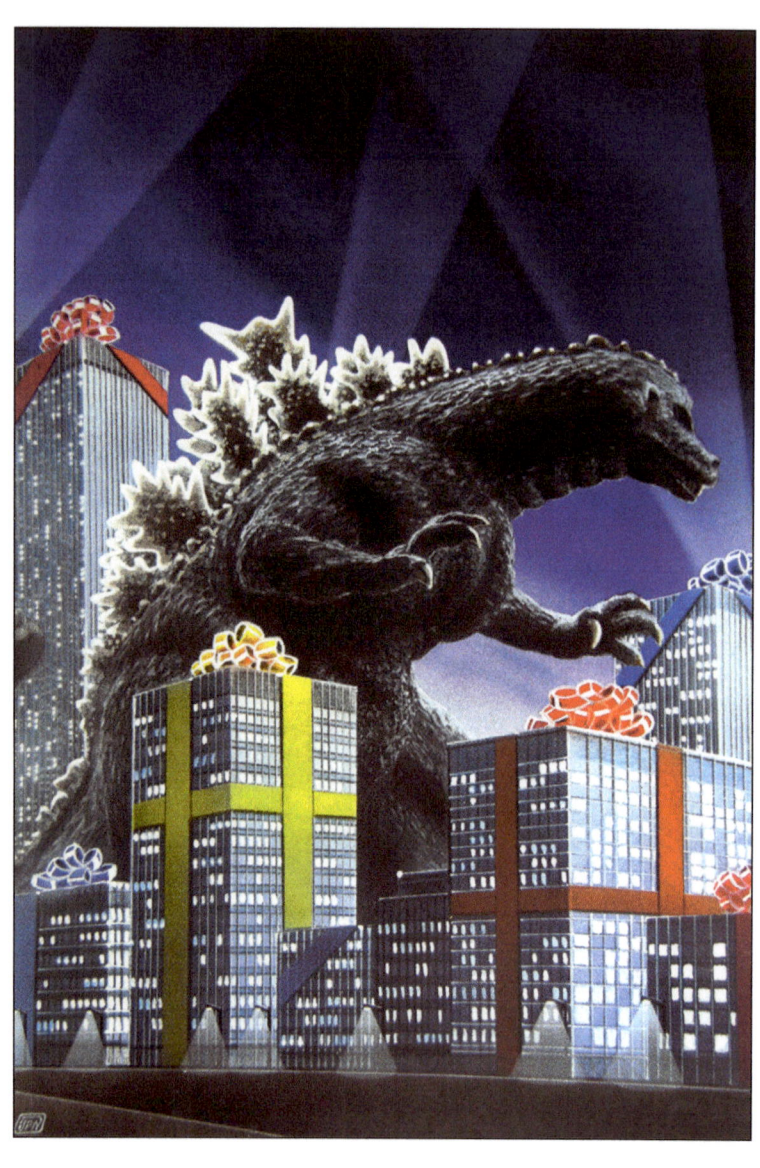

Which One Do I Open First?

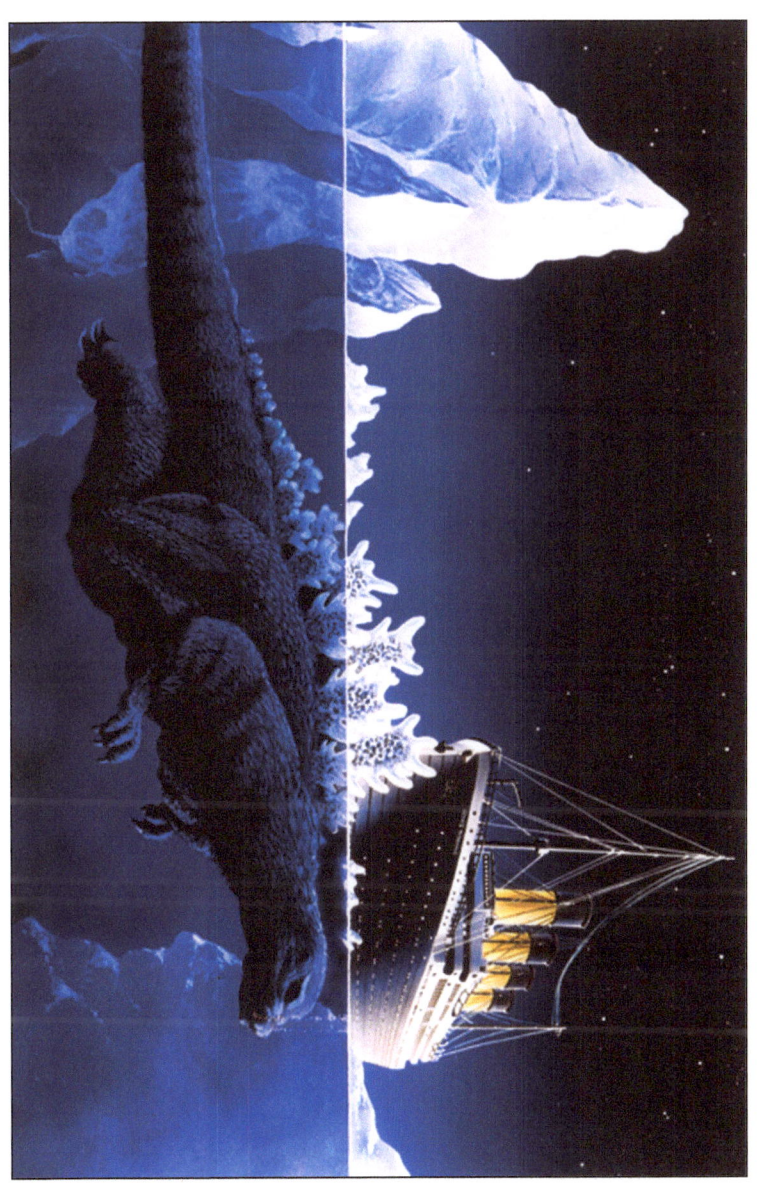

G vs T

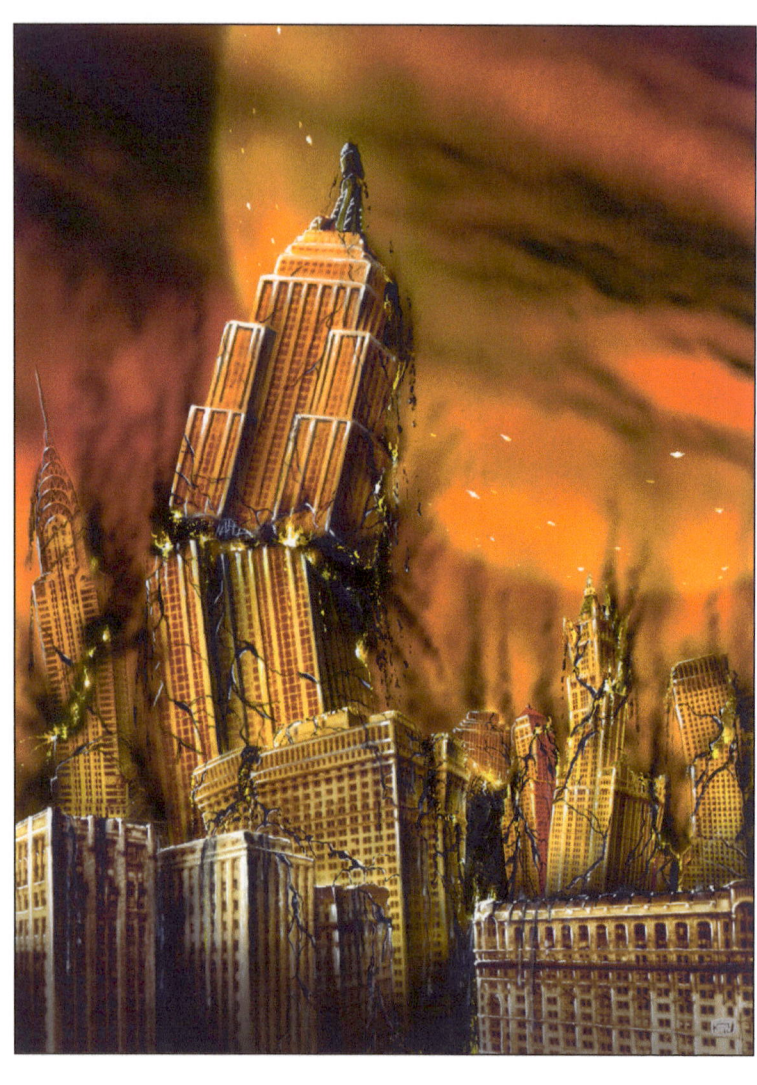

The First Passage

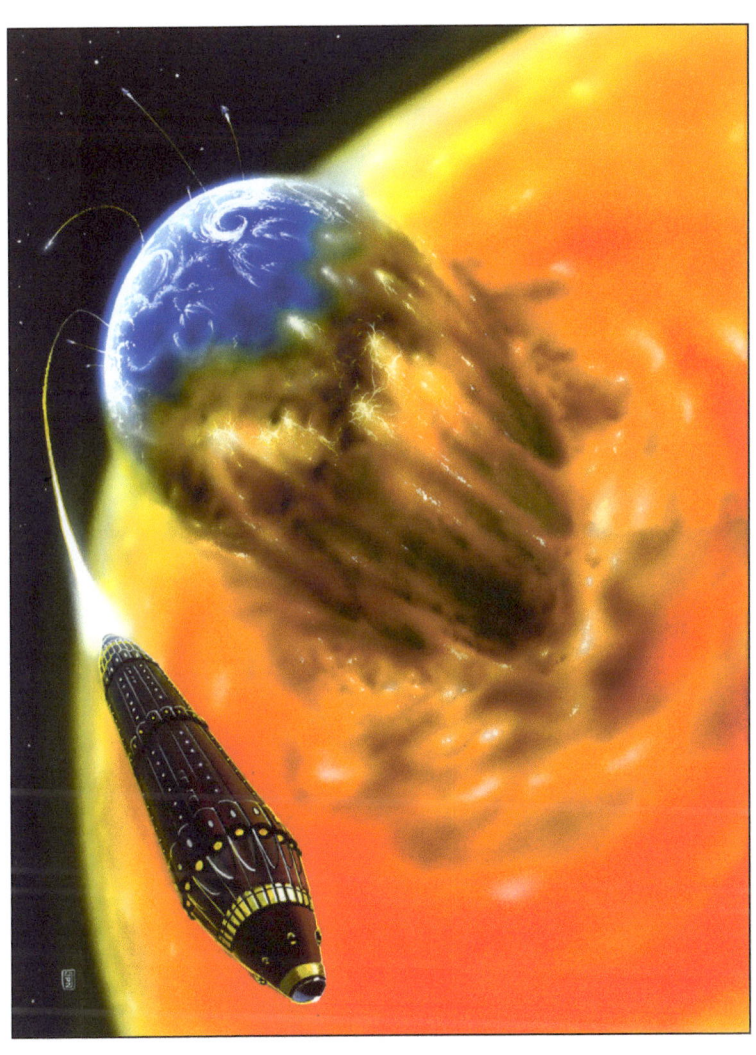

When Worlds Collide

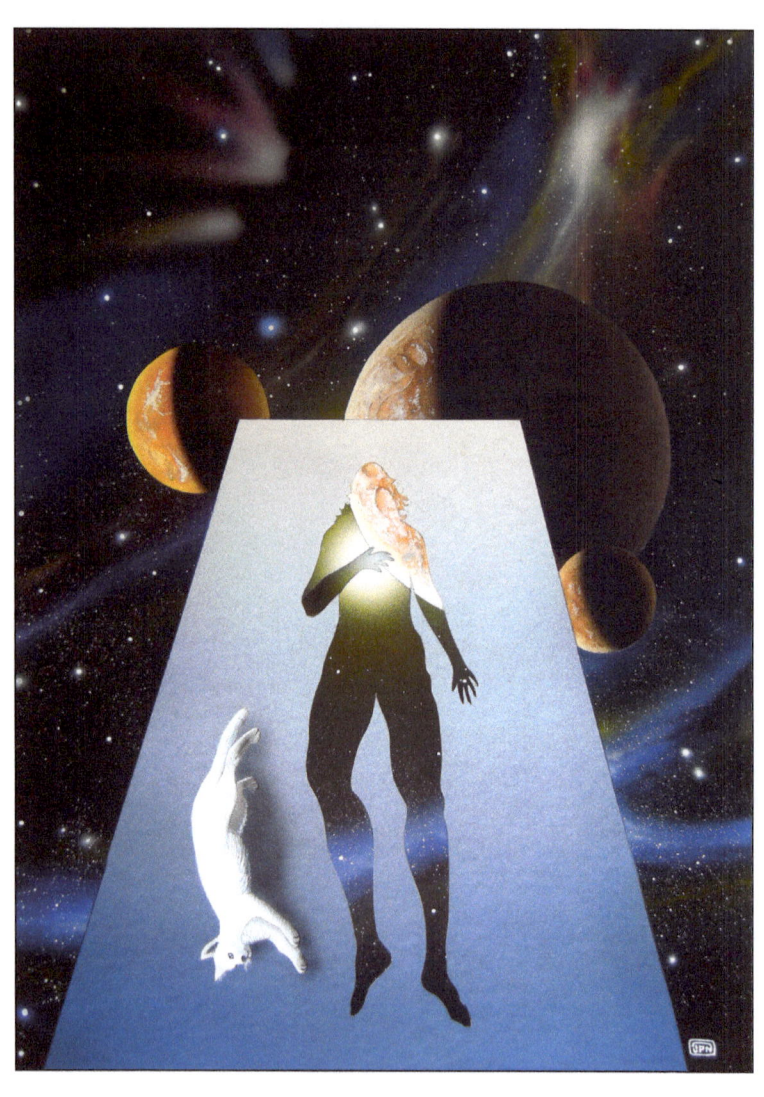

Reluctant Voyager

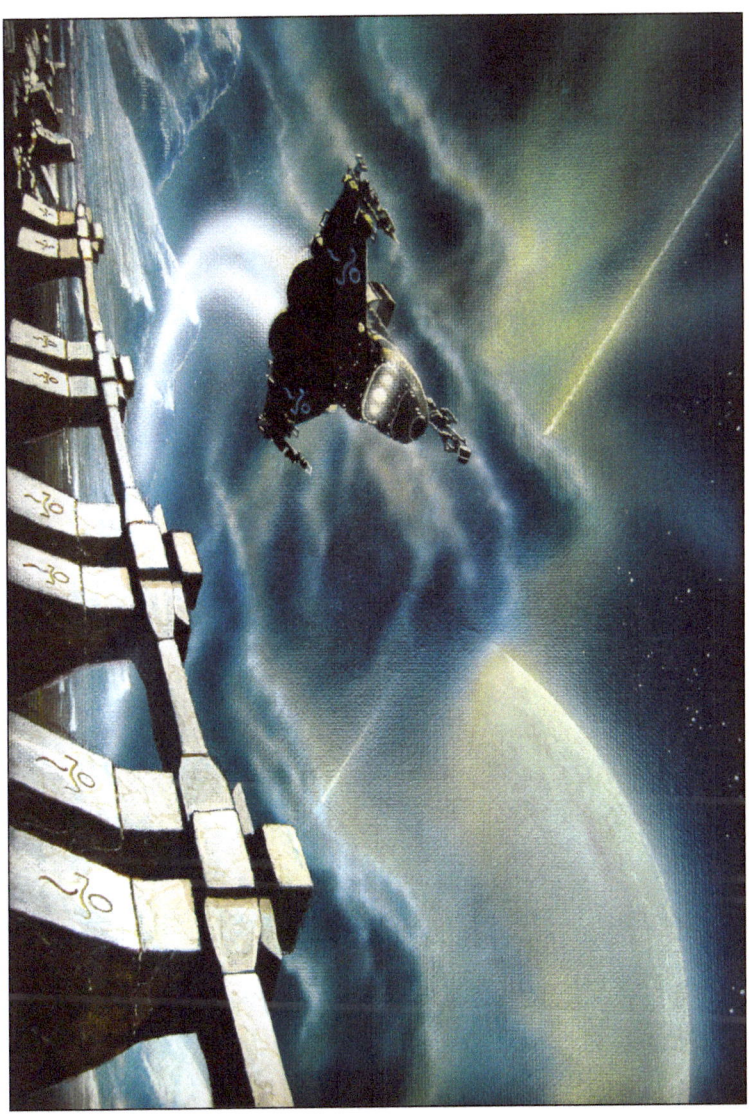

Ruins

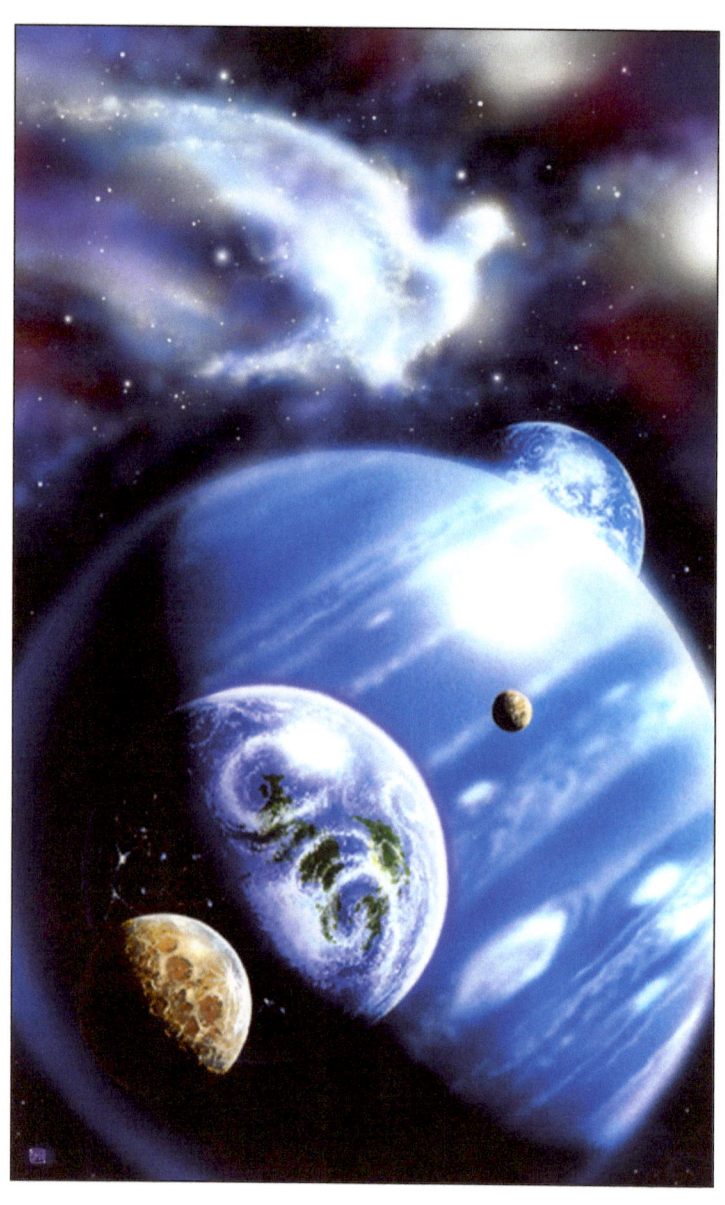

Pax Nebula

Jean-Pierre Normand is a professional illustrator, specializing in science fiction and fantasy for the past 30 years. Over two hundred book and magazine covers featuring his work has been published in Canada and the United States. He generally works in ink and liquid acrylic, applied with brush and air-brush on illustration board or canvas. His work has been shown at various conventions and other exhibits, winning several awards, notably the Aurora for artistic achievement in Canada in 1996, 1997, 1998, 1999, 2001 and 2004. His work was published in *Spectrum - The Best in Contemporary Fantasy Art*, and appeared on the covers of *Asimov's Science Fiction*, *Analog*, *On Spec* and *Science Fiction Chronicle*.

www.ingramcontent.com/pod-product-compliance
Lightning Source LLC
Chambersburg PA
CBHW040238220526
45473CB00001B/291